1-9-72

D1338266

941·152

17. NOV. 1972

-7. MAR. 1973

-6. JUN. 1973

26. JUN. 1974

(RS)

Clan Ross

The

Lowland Highlanders

by

ALAN G. R. ROBERTSON

The Story
True and Traditional
of Tain and District

095010930<del>4</del>

Printed by

HIGHLAND PRINTERS LTD., DIRIEBUGHT ROAD, INVERNESS

Contents

Illustrations

ACKNOWLEDGMENTS

I am indebted to the late Miss Williamson Ross, 22nd Chief of the Clan Ross, and Mrs Rosemary Mackenzie for articles and pamphlets relating to the Clan Ross, and to the Magistrates of Tain Town Council for permitting me to peruse the Burgh Books of Tain Town Council. I would like to thank the Edinburgh Museum for supplying the photograph of the proposed Bridge across the Dornoch Firth, and to Messrs. Simpson Bell of Hanover Street, Edinburgh, for giving me permission to use the "Clan MacKay" illustration, and to Mrs Melvin who presented me with Watson's Place Names of Ross and Cromarty, which I found indispensable.

I also must thank my daughter, Dorothy, for typing the manuscript and reading the proofs.

INTRODUCTION

Easter Ross extends from the Alness river (the River Averon) on the south, to the Dornoch Firth and Kyle of Sutherland on the north; and from east to west it stretches from Tarbat Ness to the verge of the central watershed.

The western part of this district is rather mountainous, but the eastern and seaboard areas are low-lying, being in some parts only a few feet above sea level.

It is thought that during a period of high sea level, when the glacial era was drawing to a close, the lowlands of Easter Ross were, in fact, entirely covered by sea; but later disturbances by the vast forces of nature caused the beaches to be thrown up and the sea to withdraw.

The Royal Burgh of Tain, capital of Easter Ross, is for the most part built upon an ancient raised sea beach, which subsequently became the sea margin. At that time, the tidal waters overswept the broad expanse of flat land that today spreads eastward and seaward from below the town; but as the valley glaciers finally melted, a further recession of the tide took place, and the sea fell well below its present level.

At Tain, it is traditionally believed, the Dornoch Firth became a broad valley with an easily-forded stream running through it, so narrow at one part, it is said, that a man perching himself on the over-hanging branches of a tree on the Ross-shire side of the bank, was able to hand over a parcel, by means of a long stick, to another on the opposite side. Whatever truth may be in this tale, the sea it is certain, rolled far back beyond its present bounds — but only to return again to flood what may have been a pleasant valley.

The sea, at the present day, is still spreading and encroaching upon the land. A considerable part of the shore at Tain has been swept away within living memory, and familiar landmarks in the shape of "green islands" and grassy banks, which once extended far into the Firth, have now disappeared. Old maps and legal documents confirm much of this, and show that erosion by the sea is no new problem.

A writer in the second *Statistical Account of Scotland*, referring to the Firth of Tain, observed that at low water the roots of large trees (many of them oak), were occasionally exposed by the tide far out from the shore.

It is perhaps not improbable that a greenly wooded plain may once have reached far out to the distant water's edge, but today only a bent-covered sandy flat, known as the Mhorrich Mhore, edges the Dornoch Firth. The name is descriptive, being the anglicised form of the Gaelic *A' Mhor-mhoich Mhor*, meaning "the large sea plain".

The Fendom, a more or less level tract of country, which adjoins the Mhorrich Mhore, is more productive than the latter, although the soil is in some parts sandy and light; but centuries of cultivation have turned the greater part of it into good farm land.

The name Fendom, like Mhorrich, conveys perhaps a hint of the "sea-bed" origin of these lands, for it is believed to be a corruption of Gaelic *na fana* — a term suggesting low ground of a kind liable to flooding.

The Mhorrich has long been waste land, but local legend has it that this was not always so. At one time, it is said, it was arable like the greater part of the Fendom and other lands that lie contiguous with it, but it was suddenly overwhelmed by a catastrophic sand storm, which buried crops, destroyed houses, and turned the whole area into a desert.

The fact that beads, brooches, buckles and coins dating from John Balliol to Charles II have been dug up in the vicinity, would appear to lend credence to this story; and the famous geologist Hugh Miller, who explored the ground, found evidence to suggest that the land had been quickly obliterated by sand — perhaps in a single night — as was thought to have happened at Culbin, in Morayshire.

This occurrence, if it took place, would have been comparatively recent in the history of the Mhorrich Mhore and the surrounding district, for there is evidence of the presence of man in these parts much further back in time than the earliest dated coin.

On the Mhorrich, the remains of a reindeer together with that of a dog and ox have been dug up, flint arrowheads have been found on both the Mhorrich and the Fendom, and somewhere in this neighbourhood a bronze battle-axe has been unearthed; all of which are witness of man's long association with the Dornoch Firth region; but early artifacts and historical objects have been found in various other parts of the Easter Ross lowlands, indicating that the entire *Machair* (plain) of Ross has a history which stretches far back into the distant past.

Machair Rois, the plain of Ross, lies between the Dornoch and Cromarty Firths. The Fendom and Mhorrich Mhore, already described, form part of it, and although large areas of the latter may be seen from the high ground upon which Tain stands, the *Machair*, or the greater part of it, can only be viewed from the higher ground behind the town, notably from the summit of the hill of Tain — the highest land in the parish.

The hill of Tain was once known by the more imposing name of *Ben Garrick*, but in the process of time, other generations demoted the Ben to the more humble status of "hill". Its height, it must be confessed, is a bare thousand feet, yet an extraordinary panoramic view may be obtained from its summit.

Looking eastward towards Tarbat Ness, we see the distinctive outline of the Easter Ross peninsula unfolding in front of us like a giant aerial map; on the eastern horizon we catch a glimpse of the open sea, and to the north and south respectively, are the Dornoch and Cromarty Firths, between which stretches a variegated landscape of level fields and patches of woodland.

The raised beaches, small hills and other undulations, from this distance appear flattened and ironed out; and even the hill of Nigg, the Sutors and the rising ground of the Black Isle, lose something of height in perspective and appear almost to merge with the flatter countryside.

If, however, we face about towards the west, our gaze is rewarded by a landscape of an almost abruptly different type. This is part of the hinterland of Easter Ross. All about are hills, some wooded, others heather clad and the more distant, ruggedly blue against the sky-line.

Such scenery conforms much more to the popular and romantic notion of "Clan country" than that of the low-lying lands below us; but the latter, in the days of Clans, were none the less well known and recognised Clan territory, for the majority of clansmen preferred to live in the lowlands, or in the straths, glens and more accessible uplands rather than upon inhospitable mountain tops.

The Lowlands of Easter Ross, not unnaturally, attracted a larger population than the neighbouring Highlands, for the soil was more fruitful and communications much easier.

Unfortunately, this accessibility was also a disadvantage. The land between the Firths was ever open to attack from both hill and sea, and for centuries the inhabitants of this district were forced to defend farmstead and home from the raids of freebooters and sea rovers; but constant danger bred a tough and tenacious people, who in spite of their Lowland environment, remained essentially Highland. They adhered to the Celtic law and the Celtic system of clanship and they followed their Chief to war, not only in feudal fashion as retainers and tenants, but also because they considered him to be the head of their race.

These "Lowland Highlanders", as we may call them, with their friends from the straths and glens, and a coterie of Kings, Abbots, Provosts, Pilgrims, a celebrated Celtic Saint, and a fair number of sinners, form the fabric of the story which follows.

CHAPTER I

THE NOBLE FOLK

"Out of monuments, names, words, proverbs, traditions, private records and evidences, fragments of stories, passages of books, and the like, we do save and recover something from the deluge of time."
Bacon

Although the early inhabitants of Easter Ross have left ample evidence of their presence in the number of tumuli, cairns, obelisks and other stone monuments that are found in the district, remarkably little is known about them.

Perhaps the earliest source of information about these people is Ptolemy of Alexandria, the geographer who lived in the early part of the second century A.D.

Among his works is an account of Britain, in which he locates a number of places and tribes, the position of which may now be judged with some certainty.

According to Ptolemy, a tribe called the *Decantae*, the "noble folk", lived in the district which extends from Beauly to Edderton. Why they were called "noble folk" is not clear. Their neighbours, the *Smertae*, who occupied the valleys of the Carron, Oykell and Shin, and are said to have had the rather messy and primitive custom of smearing themselves with the blood of their enemies, may have been no less estimable, as such a practice may well have been considered quite admirable in its day.

At a later period the inhabitants of these districts were known as the Picts, who through the years intermixed with the raiding and colonizing Norse and Scots. Professor Watson in *Place Names of Ross and Cromarty*, suggests that there may have been a time when Pictish, Gaelic and Norse were spoken concurrently in Easter Ross, but by the twelfth century, Gaelic had superseded both Pictish and Norse as the spoken language.

The place names of the district, however, still retain the elements of all three tongues, and although Gaelic may be said to predominate, a strong Pictish influence has persisted in some parts, noticeably in the Easter Ross seaboard area. There we find a considerable number of place-names beginning with the prefix *Pit*, such as Pithogarty, Pitnellies, Pitkerrie and Pitcalnie.

This *Pit* is considered to be Pictish, meaning a "share of land", and has been compared with, and often translated into the Gaelic *Baile*, a "stead" or "town"; thus the Gaelic equivalent of Pithogarty, "the priest's share", is *Bail' Shogartaidh*, or more properly, *Bail' an t-sagairt*, the "priest's town" (that is his manse and glebe).

There are many other place names in the district, neither Gaelic nor Norse in origin, which are thought to be Pictish, but as no Pictish literature has survived, much must remain conjecture. On the other hand, the Pictish people have left behind them very tangible evidence of their art and culture, expressed in distinctive and intricately wrought monumental sculpture. These Pictish symbol-stones, as they are often called, are mostly found in the north and eastern regions of Scotland, and in Easter Ross there are fine examples at Nigg, Shandwick and Edderton.

The Nigg stone now stands close to the west gable of the old parish church at Nigg, some distance from its original site, which was near the gate. It was blown down during a violent storm in 1727 and placed against the gable end of the church; but again it suffered misfortune towards the end of that century when it fell and was broken as it was being removed for the purpose of gaining admission to the vault of the Rosses of Kindeace. It was afterwards bound with iron straps and placed in its present position.

On one side of this stone, in a compartment at the top, are two figures resembling priests, in long robes, bending over what appears to be a table or altar, under which crouch two large dogs; and hovering above is a dove or large bird.

The remainder of this surface is occupied by a cross filled with the most intricate carving, and the spaces around the cross are decorated with raised bosses entwined by snakes. The other side of the stone is rather more weather worn, but the figure of a man in long garments, and various animal figures may be deciphered. Interlacing Celtic ornament fills up the rest.

The Shandwick stone, which stands on a hill to the west of the village of Shandwick, is also highly ornamented. On the side facing the sea is a cross decorated with raised bosses and twining snakes, in similar fashion to the Nigg stone; but in this case, the bosses — about fifty in all — appear upon the cross itself. On the spaces on each side of the shaft there are animals resembling an elephant and a lion, and underneath the cross there are panels filled with interlacing ornament. The back of the stone is divided into five panels, four of which are filled with the divergent spiral symbol, while on the fifth, the sculpture represents what may be war or hunting scenes. The animals still discernible on this side, are finely carved, but the surface of the stone is now unfortunately, very much weathered.

To the east of the Shandwick stone once stood a third stone at Hilton of Cadboll. The Hilton stone was ornately carved with symbols and contained sculpture representing horsemen, weapons of war and the hunt, but it was moved from its site about the beginning of the century, and is now housed in an Edinburgh museum.

The Nigg, Shandwick and Hilton stones are, of course, generally accepted to be the work of the Picts, but according to local tradition, they are monuments to the sons of a Danish king, who were drowned when their ship was wrecked in the Moray Firth. Their bodies were afterwards found and buried, one at Hilton, one at Shandwick, and one at Nigg; and at each of these places a sculptured stone was erected to their memory.

In one version of the story it is said that a daughter of the king of Denmark married the Thane of Ross, who brutally ill-treated and humiliated her; but by some means or other she managed to escape to Denmark and there she complained to her father, the king, of her husband's brutality. The king was naturally furious, and although it was winter-time, and the weather was adverse, he hurriedly fitted out a fleet and an army to avenge his daughter's wrongs. Three of his sons volunteered to accompany the expedition and the fleet sailed for Scotland.

As it sailed up the Moray Firth, a tremendous storm blew up and most of the vessels of the fleet either foundered or were driven ashore. The ship which carried the three princes was lost on a sunken rock off Nigg, which to this day is known as *The King's Sons*.

In the old St. Duthus cemetery at Tain, there are three horizontal stone slabs, each about 5 feet 6 inches in length, and placed side by side at slightly different levels, as if in order of precedence, which are said to mark the graves of three Danish princes slain in battle.

The similarity of this story with that of the shipwrecked princes would suggest that both have a common origin, and might in fact represent the same tradition; but this must remain surmise, as quite a number of local traditions appear to follow this pattern.

For example, at Carrieblair, Edderton, there is a Pictish standing stone which is traditionally believed to mark the grave of yet another prince.

This stone is in the shape of an obelisk about 10 feet high, upon one side of which is carved the outline of a fish above "the double disc and sceptre". It stands near the centre of a fairly large field where the Picts are reputed to have routed a strong force of Viking invaders. The leader of the Vikings, by name Prince Carius, who was killed in the battle, was buried where he fell, and the symbol-stone is said to have been erected upon the site of his grave.

Thereafter, says tradition, the field was known as *Carrieblair*, the field, or battlefield of Carius.

A shallow bay near Edderton, called Cambus-currie Bay, is said locally to have been the landing-place of Prince Carius and his fleet; but it is considered more likely that the name is derived from Gaelic, *Camus-Curaidh*, the bay of the coracle, and that Carrieblair itself is in all probability *Blar-a Charaidh*, the field of the grave plot.

It is noticeable that these traditional stories are concerned with battles between the local inhabitants, or Picts, and the Norse or Danish invaders. Few, if any tales, are told of conflict between Pict and Scot, and it may well have been that these two races either lived in a state of peaceful co-existence, or found it necessary to unite against the common enemy from across the sea.

In the parish of Logie Easter there are a number of cairns, which are said to mark the site of a great battle fought there between the Danes and the Scots, from which the adjoining burn got its name, *Allt nan Albannach*, the "Scot's burn" — now Scotsburn.

A charter of 1610 makes reference to a large cairn . . . "the cairn of stones called cairnne na marrow, alias Deid mannis cairne", and mentions also . . . "the burn called Aldain albanache, alias Scottismenis burne . . ."; and as the significantly

The Nigg Stone

By courtesy of Messrs Simpson Bell, Edinburgh

Clan MacKay

named "Dead man's Cairn" stood no great distance from other cairns in Scotsburn wood, there is little doubt that a considerable battle was fought in this area; which is further supported by some rather descriptive place-names nearby, such as *Lochan a' Chlaidheimh*, "the sword loch", and *Bearnas a' Chlaidheimh*, "sword cleft".

It is of interest to note that the burn near the field of battle became known as the Scot's burn, and was not, as one might have expected, named after the Danish invaders; which perhaps suggests that the local people who named it at the time may have regarded the Scots as incomers or strangers, in much the same way as they did the Danes; although on this occasion at least, the former must have been friendly strangers.

As Pictland once extended from the very north of Scotland to the Forth, it is perhaps not improbable that the *Albanaich* who fought at Scotsburn may have been levies or auxiliaries from lowland Scotland.

The lands of both Pict and Scot in Easter Ross, as elsewhere, were for long subject to Viking attack, but not every Norse landing was made with piratical intent, for some Norsemen came as settlers, or rather, armed colonists, and others who came to raid remained to farm. Some evidence of this is perhaps seen today in the number of farms which still bear names of Norse origin.

In certain farms such as Cadboll and Arboll, the second syllable is said to be the Norse equivalent of Gaelic, *baile*, a stead. Thus the name Cadboll is probably derived from Norse *kattar-bol*, "cat-stead"; so-called, according to one authority because the rocks facing the Moray Firth were, of old, the haunt of wild cats; and in the same way, Arboll may come from Norse, *ork-bol* meaning ark-stead.

Other farm names are of a hybrid type, part Norse and part Gaelic, of which an interesting number have the descriptive term "Meikle" in association with a Gaelic element, as in *Meikle* Rhynie and *Meikle* Daan.

Meikle (big) is said by Professor Watson to be a Norse survival, and the frequency with which it occurs in the farm names of Easter Ross would suggest that the Norse settlement in that district must have been considerable.

The Norse who settled in the eastern and more level districts of the northern Highlands, such as Easter Ross, in the course of time mixed and married with the Celtic races, adopted Gaelic, the prevailing language, and their descendants ultimately became absorbed and integrated within the Celtic Clan, and the Clan system.

The Clan Ross, whose territory once included the greater part of Easter Ross, would inevitably have received a strong infusion of Norse blood, yet every Clansman, whether by birthright or adoption, bore the common name of Ross, followed a Chief of this name and claimed a common ancestor.

The progenitor of the Rosses is said to have been *Fearchar Mac in 'T Saigart*, or Farquhar Mac-Taggart, Son of the Priest, who was created Earl of Ross about 1220.

Earl Farquhar's family name was O'Beolan or

Beolan, but he and his descendants were commonly known by their style or title of Ross.

The name Ross appears to be derived from old Gaelic or Irish, *ros*, meaning a promontory or peninsula, and the old Celtic Earls of Ross are believed to have taken their designation from the Easter Ross peninsula, or *ros*, which was an important part of their territory.

Earl Farquhar's predecessors were, in fact, Earls of *East* Ross only, for the country to the west of the watershed, now Wester Ross, was at that time known as North Argyll.

Farquhar MacTaggart was *co-arb*, or hereditary Abbot of the old Monastery of Applecross, founded by St. Maelrubbha in the seventh century. He was knighted about 1215 for his stout services to King Alexander II in crushing a revolt against the crown in Moray and Ross. Some years later he was created Earl of Ross; and as he was already Chief of the large western district from Kintail to Lochbroom (the lands of North Argyll) by acquiring the Earldom, he was the first to bring the eastern district of Ross and the western district of North Argyll under one rule.

Farquhar Ross, as we may now call him, according to traditional accounts was a man of great physical strength and courage. He was also an ardent churchman, and it was he who founded the Abbey of Fearn in 1230.

According to the second *Statistical Account of Scotland*, Earl Farquhar, about the year 1227 accompanied King Alexander II to London, where he played a notable part in the knightly pastimes of jousting and tournament.

At the English court at that time was a famous French champion, so renowned with sword and lance that the English King considered him invincible.

The indomitable Farquhar, however, challenged the Frenchman to single combat, but before entering the lists, he made a solemn vow that should he succeed in overthrowing his opponent, he would found a monastery or religious house within his own Earldom. Earl Farquhar won the encounter, and immediately set about fulfilling his vow. On his way home he called at the Priory of Whithorn, or *Candida Casa* in Galloway, and there he engaged two brothers, canons of the *Candidus Orso*, of the rule of Saint Augustus, to accompany him to the north. At the same time, he procured some relics of Saint Ninian, and with the latter, no doubt as a symbol of divine authority, and the aid of his two churchmen, he founded and endowed an Abbey at Ferne, or Fearn, in Easter Ross.

The original site of this Abbey was at Fearn at the western extremity of the parish of Edderton, but this was found to be too near the turbulent northern tribes, and in 1238 leave was granted to transfer the Abbey "for the more tranquillity, peace and quiet thereof" to its present position at Fearn, in the parish of that name. The new site, in all probability, received the name of Fearn at the time of transportation, as in old charters the Abbey is referred to as "Abbacia de Nova Farina".

Earl Farquhar continued as patron of the new Abbey, and endowed it with riches, including lands and properties, until his death in 1251. He was buried in the Abbey he had founded, and a stone effigy of a warrior with arms crossed above his breast is supposed to mark his last resting place.

Farquhar's son William, the second of the O'Beolan Earls, confirmed his father's munificence, as did most of his successors.

William, the fifth Earl, died in 1372, leaving no sons. His daughter Euphemia married Sir Walter Lesly, of Lesly, Aberdeenshire, and inherited the title of Countess of Ross in her own right. The "chiefship of the name and Clan of Ross" then passed to Earl William's brother, Hugh Ross of Rarichies. Hugh had received the lands of Rarichies from his father, the fourth Earl, killed at Halidon Hill in 1333, but he later acquired the lands of Balnagown from his brother, Earl William, and was thenceforth styled Hugh of Balnagown. He was the first of the line of Balnagown Rosses, which was to provide the Clan with their Chiefs for more than three hundred years. Sir Robert Gordon, in his *Genealogical History of the Earldom of Sutherland*, says that the family of Balnagown . . . "called themselves Rosses thereby to testify their descent from the Earls of Ross . . ." and in the same way, in accordance with Highland custom, many other people who could claim blood relationship, however remote, with the Balnagown family, adopted the name Ross as a mark of kinship with that family.

Other families with no blood ties, but who had long possessed land or property within the Earldom, and supported the family of Balnagown, looked upon themselves as Rosses, and in the course of time became Ross in name as well. In this way the Clan name spread, and the Clan grew so rapidly in numbers that according to a roll of the Clans in 1587, the name of Ross was one of the most numerous in the county. Even in the nineteenth century a writer in the *Statistical Account*, referring to the parish of Tain, says: "Most of the land-owners, and in truth most of the people, bore the name of Ross: or, to speak more correctly, almost everybody possessed two surnames, by one of which (in general a patronymic beginning with Mac) he was universally known in conversation, although he deemed himself called upon to change it to Ross, or sometimes to Munro, whenever he acquired any status in society, or became able to write his name. . . ."

At the present time, in spite of improved communications, emigration, two World Wars and a drift to the south, many of the Clan have clung to the old home, and the name of Ross is still very much to the fore in Easter Ross.

Some considerable space has been devoted to the Rosses in this chapter because of the ancient prominence of that name in Easter Ross; but other Clans have also played an important part in the history of the Ross "country".

The Clan Munro, neighbours and friends of the Rosses, had a particularly close association with Easter Ross. The Munro "country", as such, extended from the Alness river southward almost as far as Dingwall; but as the Munros also possessed lands on the Ross side of the Alness river from an early date, the Munro influence tended to be stronger in Tain and district than in the Dingwall area.

Later, the MacKenzies, who had large territories in the west and north west, acquired extensive properties in Easter Ross from the Munros, and other families in the district.

The MacLeods, Frasers and other Clans, appear on record at various periods as holding property within the Tarbat Ness peninsula; but there were also families, who did not bear a Clan name, but who had long settled in Easter Ross during the time of the O'Beolan Earls of Ross. They were Vasses (or Wasses), Tarrels, McCullochs, Denoons, Corbetts, Ferns (or Fearns), and Mitchells. All these families were staunch supporters of the Rosses, and were regarded as belonging to the Clan, although they never assumed the name of Ross.

Their lands were, for the most part, in the agricultural lowlands between Tarbat Ness and Tain, and in some cases included one-time Abbey lands, probably acquired by early family influence or connection with the Abbey of Fearn. Members of these families are known to have held office in Fearn Abbey, and at least three have held the rank of Abbot.

The family name of Fearn, or Fern, originated with the twelfth Abbot of Fearn. His name was Finlay M'Fead, but he was held in such high esteem that the King, it is said, commanded that he and his descendants should for ever more take the name of Fearn as a family surname.

Abbot Fearn, as he became known, ruled the Monastery from 1440 to 1485, and during his long and respected reign certain lands and farms, at one time belonging to the Monastery, passed into the hands of his family.

There were many descendants of the name of Fearn. David Fearn of Tarlogie, and Andrew Fearn of Pitcalzean, both of whom claimed relationship with the Abbot Fearn, and held properties that were formerly Abbey lands.

Thomas McCulloch succeeded Abbot Fearn as thirteenth Abbot; an unlucky thirteenth as it proved; for he was deprived of his charge — unjustly it is said — by Andrew Stewart, Bishop of Caithness. After this, Abbot McCulloch resided at Mid-Geanies where he erected a Chapel for himself. He died at Geanies in 1516. The McCullochs in their day were one of the most powerful families in Easter Ross. They were Barons of the Plaids — which was once a considerable estate — and they were hereditary keepers of the four Girth Crosses of St. Duthus.

The name of McCulloch appears on record in Easter Ross as early as 1368, and they owned many properties. In 1512, King James IV "granted to William McCulloch of Pladdis (Plaids), the lands of Scardy, Pladdis, Petnely, Pettogarty, Balmoduthy and Ballecarew, with the office of Bailie of the Immunity of Tane, in the Earldom of Ross and Sheriffdom of Innernys, which the said William had resigned. . . ." This would confirm that the hereditary Bailieship of Tain was in the hands of the McCulloch family at an early period. The

McCullochs appear to have had considerable influence in the Royal Burgh of Tain. Several of them held the office of Provost or chief Magistrate, and in 1660 the Provost of Tain, the senior Bailie, the Dean of Guild, and at least one other member of the Council all bore the name of McCulloch.

The Denoons were another distinguished family who probably owed something of their advancement to Church influence. The first of the name in Easter Ross was Donald Denune, Abbot of Fearn, who succeeded the martyred Patrick Hamilton as Abbot, in the year 1528. During his period of office, which lasted twelve years, the Barony of Cadboll came into his possession. These one-time Abbey lands were then feued off to the Abbot's nephew, Andrew Denoon, and the property remained in the hands of the Denoon family for several generations.

Andrew Denoon of Cadboll died during the reign of Queen Mary, and his son John, third of Cadboll, who was a Bailie of the Royal Burgh of Tain, married Katherine, sister of Alexander, ninth laird of Balnagown, in 1556. A relative, Sir David Denoon, owned considerable properties in the parish of Tain, and also the Fendom lands of Pitnellies and Pithogarty near Tain.

It is interesting to note that practically everywhere that the former adherents of Clan Ross possessed lands, old family names have persisted. There are Denoons still farming on the Fendom at the present day, and such surnames as Vass, Tarrel, Corbett and Mitchell are still relatively common in districts where the feudal families, who bore these names, once owned estates.

The Vasses were probably of Norman extraction, for the name is said to have been originally De Vallibus or Vaux. The De Vallibus family obtained lands in the province of Ross, where they became supporters not only of the Rosses, but of the Munros, for both Clans were closely associated. The Vasses certainly seem to have done their share of fighting for each Clan.

In 1500, Alexander Vass of Lochslynn fell fighting for the Munros at the battle of Druim-a'-Chait, and only about a dozen years before this, four members of the Vass family were killed while supporting the Rosses in a Clan battle against the MacKays. In 1512, King James IV "granted anew to John Vaus of Lochslyne, lands which he had earlier resigned . . .".

The Tarrels and Corbetts were among several feudal families who held lands in the Tarbat areas from the Earls of Ross. (Tarbat was once an important part of the estates of the Earls of Ross, and the district east of Portmahomack was, of old, called the "Forest of the Earls of Ross".) The land at one time known as Eister Aird, near Portmahomack, belonged to the Earls of Ross, and was granted in 1463, by John of Yle and Earl of Ross to Donald Corbat his "native esquire". This property remained in the hands of the family of Corbett for many years, and was sometimes called "Corbett's land". The supposed site of a Castle Corbet is still shown on ordnance maps.

The lands of Tarrel, also part of the Earldom of Ross, were held by a family of the same name,

Tarrel, as early as 1382. The name Tarrel was prominent in the local history of the fifteenth century, and among the signatories to an important legal document drawn up at Tain in 1439 were William de Terral and Andrew of Tarrale.

The Tarrels had family links with the McCullochs. In 1506, Angus McCulloch succeeded to the estate of Meikle Tarrel as heir to his grandmother Euphemia Tarrel; and it remained in his family until it was acquired by the Munros through the marriage of Marion McCulloch, the heiress, to George Munro of Newmore. An Alexander Tarrel was one of "the landed gentlemen of the province of Ross", slain when fighting for the Rosses at the battle Alt na Charrais, in 1487.

Alt na Charrais, where the Rosses and their allies suffered a disastrous defeat, was the outcome of a bitter feud between Clan Ross and Clan MacKay. The cause of the quarrel and the circumstances which led up to the conflict, form part of the subject of the next chapter.

CHAPTER II

PILGRIMAGE OF KING JAMES IV TO TAIN

The presence of Fearn Abbey in the Machair of Ross brought the district into some prominence, and the broad acres gifted to the Abbey by successive Earls of Ross attracted, as we have seen, a number of notable families to settle in the neighbourhood. The Abbey incumbents and clergy, although devoted to a life of prayer and meditation, also found time to take an active part in agriculture and the cultivation of the soil. They encouraged the growing of fruit and crops, so that the people of the district came to look to the Abbey not only for spiritual guidance, but for instruction and advice on farming.

The Abbey monks had also a keen economic interest in the surrounding countryside. The Abbey, for example, had milling rights which were strictly enforced, and the local tenant farmers were obliged to bring their grain to the Abbey mill at Fearn, for milling; and only for a short period in summer, when the water level in Loch Eye was too low for the water-mill, were the farmers at liberty to use their own milling stones, or querns.

Altogether, it would be true to say that in the Middle Ages, the Abbey at Fearn exerted a powerful influence upon the economic and religious life of the district; and yet, the story of the religious history of Easter Ross during this period, centres not so much around Fearn, as Tain.

Tain owes its first notice in history to perhaps the most famous of all its sons, Saint Duthus, who was born about the year one thousand in a house situated below the town, where the ivy-covered ruin of the Chapel of St. Duthus now stands. Duthus, or as he is sometimes called, Dubhthac or Duthac, is said to have been the son of high ranking parents. As a youth, he studied in Ireland. He later travelled extensively over Scotland and Ireland, where he strove to foster Christian life and education, and as he journeyed, his name became associated with many pious wonders and miracles. He died at Armagh, Ireland, on 6th March, 1065, and is described in the Irish Annals as "Chief Confessor of Scotland and Ireland". In June, 1253, his body was exhumed and brought from Ireland to Tain "quhar he was borne".

It was probably at this time that the Chapel was built upon the site of his birthplace, for it was never a parish church but a memorial cell to house the last relics of the Saint. In charge was a resident hermit whose duty it was to guard the shrine and the relics.

These relics were apparently the mystic shirt of St. Duthus, which was accredited with supernatural powers, and the Saint's skull and breast-bone; the one set in silver, and the other in gold. The bones of St. Duthus were reputed to have marvellous curative powers, and many people with bodily infirmities resorted to Tain in the hope of obtaining a miracle cure, in the same way as pilgrimage is made to Lourdes at the present day.

The name of St. Duthus was so revered in mediaeval times that even the kings of Scotland made pilgrimage to Tain to do homage and penance at the shrine of the Saint. Both Alexander III and James III are said to have visited the town, but the most regular royal visitor to Tain was King James IV. He appears to have made regular pilgrimages to Tain every year for at least twenty successive years, from 1492-1513.

Tain, in the days of the pilgrimages, was not only prominent as an Immunity or Free Burgh, but it was also privileged as a "Girth" or "Sanctuary". A Girth or Sanctuary was a territory which had the protection of the Church, and by favour of the King, where all who fled there from arrest or persecution, could claim asylum, and were free from arrest as long as they remained within the defined limits of this territory. In the case of Tain, this area was marked by four Girth crosses placed around the boundaries of the town. The holy Girth of Saint Duthus was, in fact, nearly as large as the parish of Tain.

The Sanctuary was, for the most part, observed with superstitious awe and respect, but on at least two occasions it was subjected to desecration and violence.

In the year 1306, King Robert the Bruce, who had suffered many reverses of fortune, was forced to flee to the small island of Rathlin, off the Irish coast, while his Queen and his daughter Marjorie took refuge in the castle of Kildrummy in Aberdeenshire; but fearing an attack on the castle by the force of King Edward, they left the castle and came north to

Tain, with ladies of the court, squires and a number of knights. There they hoped to find security within the Girth, but unhappily, William Earl of Ross was at that time a supporter of the English faction, and with cynical disregard for the right of Sanctuary, he swept into Tain with a band of armed retainers, overpowered the Queen's escort, and captured the Queen and the Princess Marjorie. He carried them off with him and later surrendered them into the hands of Edward of England.

In the following year, however, the Earl of Ross and King Robert the Bruce came to an agreement, and Bruce sealed the reconciliation by giving his sister, the Princess Maud, in marriage to the Earl's son Hugh. From then onwards, the Earl of Ross became a trusted friend and supporter of King Robert, and at the battle of Bannockburn he led the men of Ross, Sutherland and Caithness. His younger son, Sir Walter, was killed during the battle.

Bannockburn was one of these rare occasions when the northern clans fought as a united force in battle. More often than not they were at loggerheads and were frequently warring and feuding with each other.

In the fifteenth century, the Highlands were in such a turmoil that King James I of Scotland attempted to curb the Highland Clans by a stratagem. In 1427, he summoned all the most important Chiefs in the north to a Parliament in Inverness. Of these, about forty turned up, and for their pains were promptly seized by order of the King, tried, then imprisoned, hanged, beheaded or banished, according to the supposed enormity of their crimes.

This rough justice did not seem to have much effect, for some of the wilder clansmen refused to be intimidated, and carried on their predatory habits with scant regard for the King's law.

Among these was a certain Thomas MacKay, or MacNeill, of Creich, a kinsman of Angus Dubh MacKay of Strathnaver (one of the Chiefs held captive by James). Thomas MacKay had a feud with Mowatt, laird of Freswick in Caithness and the two came to blows, when Mowatt, who had strayed far from his home territory, was making his way north through Sutherland. Mowatt lost the encounter and fled the field with the remnants of his following; but as the victors barred his retreat to the north, he made for Easter Ross in the hope of finding asylum within the Immunity of Tain. The Girth was reached, but so close was the pursuit that the fugitives sought what they believed would be greater security within the very walls of St. Duthus Chapel. Thomas MacKay and his henchmen, however, flushed with victory, were in no mood to be baulked of their prey, so they set fire to the thatched roof of the Chapel, burning all who had taken refuge, thus technically evading the right of Sanctuary by destroying their enemies without seizing them on sacred ground.

This second violation of the sacred Girth of St. Duthus was too much for King James, who immediately ordered a proclamation to be issued denouncing Thomas MacKay as a rebel, and promising lands and possessions to anyone who would kill or capture him.

A year later MacKay was caught and hanged at

Inverness; just retribution for a Highland cateran; but small consolation for the people of Tain, who lost not only their famous Chapel, but certain priceless parchments relating to the early constitution of the town, which had been lodged there for safe keeping.

The burning of Tain's early charters left the burgh open to attack by other burghs who disputed its ancient rights and privileges. These attacks were, of course, stoutly resisted by the inhabitants of Tain, and after some years of wrangling, an appeal was made for legal investigation into the whole matter. According to a copy of a legal document, now in the possession of the Tain Town Council, a jury authorised by the Earl of Ross, and consisting of the leading men of Ross, the Sheriff of Inverness and a burgess of that town, sat in 1439 to decide the issue.

The presence of the Inverness men on the jury would suggest no bias in favour of Tain, yet the finding was that Tain was founded as an Immunity by ". . . a certain most illustrious king of Scots, Malcolm Canmore of good memory", and had ". . . full and free power of buying and selling all goods whatsoever within the four corner crosses of the said Immunity and that they never have paid, nor of right do pay, any contribution to the Kings of Scotland nor to the Earls of Ross except the custom of our lord the King."

This document, it would seem, firmly established that Tain as an Immunity had not only the freedom of trade, but also freedom from the exactions of neighbouring lords and others.

Outside the burgh, the state of affairs was not so happy, as Easter Ross, like many other parts of Scotland during the early part of the fifteenth century, was at times subjected to the rapacity of lawless men who forcibly extorted their own form of levy.

Sir Robert Gordon in his *Earldom of Sutherland* tells of a bandit leader, by name Donald Ross, who carried on a thieving trade in Easter Ross round about the same time as the destruction of St. Duthus Chapel, and although the story is probably largely apocryphal it is illustrative of the barbarity of the age.

Ross, according to Sir Robert Gordon, in the course of his reiving activities carried off two cows belonging to a poor woman. The woman, on seeing the animals being driven away, screamed out in despair that she intended to walk barefooted to the court of King James to have justice done, and that she would not wear shoes again until she had made her complaint in person. This so enraged Ross that he roared out that he would make sure she was properly shod to make the journey to the court. He then ordered the woman to be seized, and two horse shoes were fixed to her feet with nails driven into her flesh. In spite of this inhuman treatment the woman in time recovered, and as soon as she was able to travel she went to the King and complained of the outrage. The King gave the aggrieved woman a sympathetic hearing, then immediately ordered a warrant to be sent to the Sheriff of Ross, demanding that the bandit be brought to trial without delay. Donald Ross was soon run to earth, and with twelve of his followers, was dragged under heavy escort to Perth, where the Court was then held.

After the formality of a trial, all were condemned. In the words of Sir Robert Gordon ". . . Mack-Donald Rosse being brought out of prissone with tuelve of his associats, the king commanded that they should be likewise shod with iron shoes, in the same sort as they had before served the woman and afterwards, that they should be caried thrie severall dayes through the streets of Edenburgh, for a spectacle to the people. All of which being performed, the said MackDonald Rosse was beheaded, and his tuelve companions hanged on the high wayes. A notable paterne of justice, which may be an example to the negligent and sluggish justiciars of our tyme, who suffer the poore and weak to be oppressed by strong and idle wagabounds."

Donald Ross, who received and undoubtedly merited this "notable paterne of justice", we may hope did not run to pattern. He was undoubtedly a black sheep among his Clan Ross contemporaries, as the Clan, through force of circumstances, were not given to reiving. Living as they did, in comparatively rich agricultural country, they were more occupied with the defence of their own lands than in making incursions into others, for the low-lying Easter Ross lands constantly invited the attention of robbers and cattle lifters.

For long, the Rosses had to contend with sporadic raids, but before the fifteenth century ended they became embroiled with the MacKays of Strathnaver in full-scale Clan warfare, and this quarrel was destined to last intermittently for upwards of fifty years.

It began with Angus Roy MacKay, restless and warlike Chief of MacKays of Strathnaver, who made repeated forays into "Ross country", killing, burning and carrying off booty. His last act of depredation took place somewhere in the Portmahomack area about the year 1481, when he and his men suffered defeat at the hands of a determined force of Easter Ross men.

Angus Roy and some of his followers, in retreat, sought refuge in the church at Tarbat; but as in the case of the refugees in the Chapel of Saint Duthus, more than half a century previously, no mercy was shown. Neither the sanctity of the church, nor the fact that Angus Roy MacKay and Alexander Ross of Balnagown were related, stayed the wrath of the exasperated Easter Ross men. They set fire to the church and left Angus Roy and his followers to perish in the blaze.

Angus Roy had a son too young to assume the duty of avenging his father's death; he was bound by the Clan code of honour to do so; but as soon as he was old enough he applied for help to John, Earl of Sutherland, for assistance in carrying out an attack on the Rosses. The Earl sent his uncle, Robert Sutherland, with a picked force; and on the 11th of July 1487, John Riabhaich MacKay at the head of his Clan, and his Sutherland allies, invaded Strathoykell, wasting it with fire and sword. Strathoykell was Ross territory, and when the news of the raid reached Alexander Ross of Balnagown, he gathered his clansmen and hastened to meet the raiders.

The clans met at Alt na Charrais, a small tributary of the Oykell, and there, in the words of Sir Robert Gordon, "ensued a cruell battell, which continued a long space, with incredible obstinacie; the doubt

of the victorie being no less than wes the desyre;
much blood wes shed. In the end, the inhabitants of
Rosse, being unable to indure the enemies force,
were utterly disbanded and put to flight. Alexander
Rosse, laird of Balnagowne wes there slain with
seaventeen other landed gentlemen of the province
of Rosse, besyds a great number of commoun
souldiers."

The loss of their Chief appears to have decided
the day against the Rosses, and as no quarter was
given, their losses were very severe.

The Kalendar of Fearn gives the name of some
of the gentlemen who were killed in the conflict. In
addition to Alexander Ross of Balnagown, they
were William Ross of little Allan, Alexander Tarrel,
Angus McCulloch of Tarrel, John Vass, William
Vass, Thomas Vass, Hutcheon Vass, John Mitchell
and William Ross.

For those of the name of Vass, Alt na Charrais
appears to have been particularly tragic, but it was
a disaster for the whole Clan Ross. Lands were
ravaged, houses burned and families scattered; yet
Clan Ross though weakened by the defeat, was not
crushed, and was able to dispute with the MacKays
and others for years to come.

Under the leadership of their new Chief, Sir David
Ross of Balnagown, they carried on warring and
feuding to such effect that Sir David Ross and Ian
Roye MacKay were summoned to appear before
the Earl of Argyll — at that time Lord High
Chancellor of Scotland — to give assurance of the
future good conduct of their Clans. Each of them
extended his hand to the Chancellor and swore to

keep peace in the King's name, so that their "folkis sal be harmless and skaithless"; and they bound themselves to pay a penalty of five hundred merks should they fail to keep their pledge. Their vow, for what it was worth, was soon broken and the feud was renewed. MacKay forays continued well into the sixteenth century, and only ceased when that brave and warlike Clan found themselves fully occupied nearer home, in their turn defending their "country" from the predatory onslaughts of their Sutherland and Caithness neighbours.

During this long period of Clan warfare, the Immunity of Tain, apart from Thomas MacKay's lapse, seems to have been carefully respected. The burning of the Chapel of St. Duthus apparently did little to destroy confidence in Tain as a place of Sanctuary, for fugitives from oppression, violence, or even justice, still continued to arrive within the Girth. Some, including those in high places, sought political asylum there, and even the King, or his chosen representatives, hesitated to enforce authority.

One of the most noted of these political refugees was William, Lord Crighton, who fled to Tain in 1483. Crighton, a man of great importance during the reign of James III, became involved in political intrigue, and was suspected by the King of holding treasonable correspondence with England. Knowing he was suspect, Crighton thought it prudent to make a hasty leave of the political scene, and to take refuge within the Girth of St. Duthus.

In Tain, he found accommodation at the house of the vicar of St. Duthus, but there he was followed by the King's macer, who, in the presence of two local bailies, summoned him to appear at Edinburgh. Lord Crighton, however, refused to leave Tain, wisely deciding to stay with his host the vicar. He was outlawed in the following year, and his estates forfeited, but as long as he remained within the area of the four Girth crosses, he knew his life was safe.

Lord Crighton continued to live within the bounds of Tain for a number of years until he was, at length, persuaded to meet King James at Inverness and crave the royal indulgence, but although a partial reconciliation was made, he was not restored to favour, and about a year later he died at Tain in abject poverty. His dust, like that of others once renowned, may lie today in an unnamed grave within the shadow of the Church of St. Duthus.

This Church, which was built and dedicated to St. Duthus in the fourteenth century, six or seven decades before the destruction of the Chapel, was looked upon with great reverence. Relics of St. Duthus, which appear to have survived the fire in the Chapel were placed here, and attracted pilgrims from all over Scotland.

King James III lavished gifts upon St. Duthus Church, and procured from the Pope and the Bishop of Ross sanction for converting it into an ecclesiastical college, with a new and larger personnel consisting of a provost, five canons, two deacons, a sacrist with an assistant clerk, and three choristers — all being liberally endowed by the King out of Crown lands.

The constitution was established in 1487, in the

same year as the disaster at Alt na Charrais, and only a matter of months before James himself met tragic death at Sauchieburn.

In the following year, the young James IV came to the throne. He continued royal tradition by contributing generously to the Church of St. Duthus, and he directed that an annual sum be paid from the royal treasury to the Chaplain of St. Duthus, for the purpose of saying masses on behalf of his late father's soul.

As he grew older, the young King paid frequent penitential visits to the Shrine of St. Duthus at Tain, seeking perhaps to atone for his complicity in the rebellion which had led to the death of his father.

Apart from its fourteenth-century Collegiate Church, and the old Chapel near the links, Tain possessed yet another parish Church of an earlier unknown date, dedicated to St. Duthus. This stood near the present-day Church of St. Duthus, and part of it still remains in the shape of the small Chapter House alongside.

James IV visited, it would seem, all three churches, although the old Chapel must have then been roofless.

In the Royal treasurer's accounts for 1504, the following entries show that on the 23rd of October of that year the King made an offering of 14s. "in Sanct Duchois chapell quhair he was borne" (the old chapel near the link); also, "in Sanct Duchois chapell in the kirkyard of Tayne" (which probably refers to the older, or original parish church); and also, "in Sanct Duchois Kirk" (that is the collegiate church as distinguished from the parish church).

The King set great store upon a "relict of St. Dutho", which was preserved as having miraculous healing powers, and which continued in the hands of his son James V for many years.

James IV was a very popular pilgrim on his northern sojourns, and when his mood was not blackly penitential he was gay and sociable, loving music and good company. On these occasions he would ride at the head of a splendid cavalcade, accompanied by musicians, entertainers and the court jester. On one such journey, in 1504, he was accompanied by a poet, three falconers, four Italian minstrels and a Moorish drummer; and, according to the royal treasurer's accounts, he did not lack entertainment by the way.

There was paid "to the madinnis of Forres that dansit to the king, 9s."; "to the madinnis that dansit at Elgin siclyke, 9s. 6d."; and "to the madinnis that dansit at Darnaway, 14s.": not perhaps conventional behaviour on a visit of penance, yet it is said that there was no more zealous religionary in the country than James. He ate no meat on Wednesdays or Fridays; he would not mount a horse on Sunday, even to go to Mass, and he would hear two masses before doing any serious business. Nothing was allowed to interfere with his annual pilgrimage to the Shrine of St. Duthus; and sometimes, in sombre mood, leaving his retinue behind, James, they say, would walk alone in all humility, with head uncovered and feet bare, through the streets of Tain to the Shrine of St. Duthus.

On one occasion, he travelled alone from Stirling to Tain without hindrance. That he was able to travel through such wild country unharmed was a measure of his popularity, for it was his force of personality rather than the rigour of his law that kept the Highlands quiet. According to Bishop Leslie, "The haill realm of Scotland was in sic quietness that the King rade him allane with great diligence on ane day from Striveling to Perth, and Aberdeen to Elgin in post, quhair he reposit him on ane hard burd ane certain space of nycht, in Mr. Thomas Leslie's house, the parson of Kingussie, and in the morn raid to Sanct Duchois, in Rosse, to masse, the last day of August, but returnit again to Strivling to tournay, accompanyit with the nobilitie of these cuntries."

The Royal treasurer's accounts of the day give some intimate details of the King's expenditure on his visits to Tain. For example, in 1501, 5s. was given to the "Hermit of Sanct Duchois Chapell", indicating that the chapel which marked the birth place of St. Duthus, though in ruins, was still in the custody of a local hermit.

In 1504, the King's beneficence included an offer made "at the stok of Sanct Duchois town", and a gratuity "to the man that bore Sanct Duchois bell"; and in 1511, there was paid "to ane pardonar with Sanct Duthous Crouss, 2s."

James IV paid his last visit to Tain in 1513, and his expenses, as recorded by his treasurer, read: "Aug. 4. Item for three bonets to the King the tyme he past to Sanct Duchois, 36s. Aug. 8. Item to the King's grace when he past to Sanct Duchois, £66."

A month later he fell on the field of Flodden.

His son James V is presumed to have made at

least one pilgrimage to Tain, and is traditionally believed to have walked barefooted through the streets of Tain, as his father is said to have done.

The route, or bridle path taken by the Royal visitors at the approaches of Tain is known as the King's Causeway, and vestiges of the original, which still exist, are pointed out to this day.

According to local tradition, this part of the causeway was hurriedly built with stones over a peat bog by the people of Tain when they heard that a Royal pilgrim was approaching in his bare feet.

The King's Causeway, Upper King Street, and the narrow street leading to the High Street, known as King Street, together constitute the major part of what may be called Tain's "Royal two miles", and were so named to commemorate the once intimate connection of the old burgh with the Stewart kings.

During the reign of King James V, Patrick Hamilton, titular Abbot of Fearn, was burned at St. Andrews as a heretic. He was the first preacher of the Reformation in Scotland, and though probably never resident at Fearn, his martyrdom excited feeling in the countryside around his Monastery, and perhaps hastened the "wind of change" which even then was stirring in the north.

One important churchman, Sir Nicolas Ross, Provost of the Collegiate Church of St. Duthus, who was appointed Abbot of Fearn in 1549, very soon openly embraced the Protestant faith. He was a kinsman of Alexander Ross of Balnagown, who also cast his lot with the Reforming party about this time, and although from evidence it would appear that the latter was probably of no strong religious conviction, his example must have had considerable influence.

Nicolas Ross as Provost of Tain and Abbot of Fearn attended Parliament in 1560 with Sir Robert Munro of Foulis, when the Scottish Parliament met to repudiate the supremacy of Rome.

After 1560 the Church of St. Duthus came into use for the reformed worship, and a fine oaken pulpit was presented to the Church by the Regent Murray, friend of John Knox, in recognition of the "zeal of the people of Tain in the cause of the Reformation".

As the old beliefs decline so did the importance of Tain as an Immunity, for with the new teachings came a waning in faith in the magical properties of the relics of St. Duthus; and in consequence a falling off in the number of pilgrimages to his Shrine at Tain.

This, in the end, meant a serious loss of prosperity for the Burgh, but the people of Tain, with apparent disregard for their material interests, whole-heartedly supported the cause of the Reformers, and in so doing, hastened the end of a great era in the history of their Burgh.

The relics of St. Duthus, the skull and breast-bone, and the Saint's "fertyr", or portable shrine, were carried off to Balnagown for safe-keeping by Sir Nicolas Ross just before he left for Edinburgh in 1560. He got a receipt for them, which is still in existence, and in this, the monetary value is assessed at 2,000 merks (about £120 sterling).

Thereafter, nothing further is heard or seen of the relics.

CHAPTER III

LAWLESS HIGHLAND LAIRDS

James IV's death at Flodden deprived Scotland of a strong and popular ruler, and during the minority of his son, James V, there were troubles and disturbances in the north.

Easter Ross was at this time comparatively unaffected by Clan warfare, as the old adversaries of Clan Ross were busy elsewhere; but there was no lack of lawlessness and strife among local lairds.

The Highland laird, or baron, remote from central authority, often exercised almost despotic power over his tenants and workers, or for that matter of it, over any who passed through his lands. He held his own courts, passed his own judgements, and could punish by fine or forfeiture, or even inflict the death penalty by hanging or drowning (*furca et fossa*).

One of the most notorious of these sixteenth-century lairds was Andrew Beg Munro, third of Milton. He was the very personification of the big bad baron of fiction. Ferocious and ruffianly, he was known as Black Andrew of the seven castles; but whether he was known as Black Andrew from his personal appearance, or from the cruel actions with which tradition associates his name, is not clear.

If tradition is true then his record of crimes is

indeed black. It is said that he had a callous disregard for life, and that he murdered with his own hand, eight of his tenants — all heads of families — who had incurred his displeasure. He is also reputed to have caused the death of an old woman under particularly gruesome circumstances. When the disputed marches between the adjoining properties of Milton and Balnagown were being fixed, this old woman gave evidence against Munro in Balnagown's favour. The wrathful Black Andrew then caused a pit to be dug, and buried the woman alive, with her head down. He is also said to have used his power of pit and gallows to the full. Those who crossed his path were dealt with in summary fashion. Unfortunate men who dared to offend, were hung from the gallows, and women victims were drowned in a pool.

The gallow-hill of the Barony of Milton is situated on the march between Milton and Balnagown, near the old Logie Free Church manse, and the drowning pool is adjacent to the manse. Here in 1864, while excavations were being made in connection with the Highland Railway, many human bones were dug up; and some years previously, a large quantity of human bones were dug up on the site of Milton Castle; and these, the credulous were inclined to believe, were none other than the remains of the victims of Black Andrew Munro.

It should be remembered, however, that as Black Andrew was hereditary Bailie or Mayor of Ross, during part of James V's minority, by the nature of his office he would have to exercise great severity because of the then lawless state of the country, and his fierceness would no doubt have been exaggerated with the years until he acquired the reputation of being something of an ogre. There can be no doubt, however, that he was a very violent character, and a time-honoured story is told of his fitting and dramatic end.

According to this, Black Andrew during harvest time, exercising his feudal authority, summoned all the women of his estates to appear for work in the harvest field. When they had all gathered at Milton, the tyrant, who had been drinking heavily, gave orders that the women should strip and work stark naked in the fields. He then returned to the castle and his bottle, and it was very much later before he gave even a thought to the poor women toiling outside in the chill autumn evening. Suddenly, he jumped to his feet and hurried out to ensure that his orders had been carried out to the full; but such was his condition that he staggered as he went, then slipped down the steps of the castle and broke his neck.

Black Andrew's seven castles were situated at Delny and Newmore, in the parish of Rosskeen, Contullich and Kildermorie, in the parish of Alness, Dochcarty in the parish of Dingwall, Culnaha in the parish of Nigg, and of course, Milton in Kildary. The castle of Milton was built by Andrew Munro's grandfather, John, brother of the fourth laird of Foulis, during the second half of the fifteenth century. When he first began the building, Alexander Ross, laird of Balnagown strenuously objected, and threatened to prevent him completing it. Munro countered the threat by calling in the help of John,

Earl of Sutherland. He appealed to the Earl to "support and defend him against the Rosses", and in the words of Sir Robert Gordon . . . "John Earl of Sutherland was a great supporter and defender of the Munros, and particularlie the familie of Miltoun, whom he manteyned against the laird Balnagowan; and when the Munros began to build first the house of Milntoun, Earl John went himselff in persone, to defend them against Balnagown his braging, who indeavoared to stop and hinder them from building the castell. Then, returning home into Southerland, he left a company of men at Milntoun for the defence against the Rosses, vntil the most part of the castell wes finished; which kyndnes the Munroes of Milntoun do acknowledge vnto thes day. . . ."

This squabble must have strained the good relationship that usually existed between the Clans Ross and Munro, but as George Munro of Foulis, brother of John Munro who built the castle, married a daughter of the laird of Balnagown, the trouble must have blown over.

Alexander Ross, ninth chief of Balnagown, was another turbulent sixteenth-century laird. He lived during the Reformation period, when the Highlands were in a particularly unsettled state, and his misdeeds all but matched some of these perpetrated by the renowned Black Andrew.

It will be recalled that when Nicolas Ross, Abbot of Fearn, and Robert More Munro, Baron of Foulis, represented Easter Ross at the first Reformed Parliament of 1560, Alexander Ross of Balnagown had also taken the side of the Reformers, perhaps, as has been said, more from self interest than from any real religious conviction; for with the decay of the old church he no doubt saw an opportunity of obtaining some of the old Abbey lands which his ancestors, the Earls of Ross, had given away so liberally.

The revenues of Fearn Abbey were very great, but even before 1560, certain Abbey lands were being feued off to friends and relatives of the Abbots. Later, the local barons appear to have put some pressure upon the clergy, and Thomas Ross, "Commendator" of the Abbey of Fearn, and successor to Nicolas Ross, the Abbot who had voted with the Reformers, was forced to leave the district and reside for a number of years in Forres, during which time he received little or no benefit from the revenues of the Abbey. The masterful Alexander Ross of Balnagown was very likely one of the barons who had brought pressure to bear upon his clansman, Thomas Ross. Certainly in the year 1562 he "persuaded" three canons of the Monastery of Fearn to witness a document which assigned some of the Abbey lands in his favour. This they later asked to be revoked, alleging "in the presence of the commendator Nicolas Ross abbot of Ferne" that Alexander Ross of Balnagown "by threats and force" compelled them against their will to subscribe to the document, and that "they signed the said pretended charter on account of fear, in terror, and against their will."

Ten years later Alexander's persuasive methods were again in evidence when he raided the lands of Alexander Innes of the Plaids. Innes, whom it appears had acquired the hereditary Bailieship of Tain from the McCullochs, "agreed" to resign into Alexander Ross's hands ". . . ye toune and lands of Cadboill wt ye fortalice yairoff, Petcandie, Skardii wt ye miln, Petogartye, Petnilie, Plaidis etc . . . wt ye heretable office of ye Bailserie Of Tayne." Alexander of Balnagown next destroyed Innes's tower of Cadboll and imprisoned Innes. Later, James Earl of Morton, Regent of Scotland, summoned him to appear at a Parliament at Edinburgh "ffor ye doune casting of ye battelet towr of Catboll and ye allegit taking and presoning of Alexander Innes of Plaids and Catboll. . . ."

Balnagown ignored the summons so he was declared rebel and "put to the horn". He was at length imprisoned in Tantallon Castle, but on signing an agreement that he would live peaceably, he was set free. Not long after his return he was once again disturbing the peace of the district, but this time his defiance of the government resulted in letters of fire and sword being issued against him, and his own son George was charged with the task of pursuing and apprehending him.

Alexander, however, refused to be suppressed, and in 1588 we hear of a complaint being made against him for seizing the Chapter House in St. Duthus churchyard, and making use of it as his girnell and larder, and other "prophain usis and keipis". The King in Council ordered the said Alexander Ross to "ceis from furder occupeing . . . and redd himself guids and geir therefrae." Whether he did or not is not recorded. Alexander died in 1592.

In 1597 the Abbacy of Fearn was erected into a

barony called the "Barony of Geanies", and given by James VI to Sir Patrick Murray, who was a favourite of his. According to the second *Statistical Account* ". . . this grant did not prove a very advantageous one, for the whole of the lands contained in it, having either violently or by feus from the latter Abbots, been kept possession of by the neighbouring gentlemen, he found it so difficult to recover them that he accepted 18,000 merks Scots from the laird of Balnagown and his son in law, Sinclair of Mey, for the whole Barony."

This indicates fairly graphically how the local lairds had benefited from the spoils of the Reformation; but not all the emoluments and chaplainaries went to the lairds; some, as John Knox had intended it, were converted into bursaries to help young men to study at the Universities. One of these bursars was John Munro, a nephew of Sir Robert More Munro of Foulis, who had voted in the Reformation Parliament.

In 1605, King James VI prohibited the meeting of the General Assembly of the Church. Nevertheless, some of the presbyteries, of which Tain was one, appointed members to attend it. The minister of Tain at that time was the bursar John Munro, and he and other eighteen ministers met at Aberdeen and duly constituted a General Assembly. They were summoned to appear before the Privy Council, and seventeen of them obeyed. Ten repented, but the remainder refused to submit, and John Munro was one of the latter. He maintained stoutly that the Assembly at Aberdeen was "a verie lawful General Assembly".

For this, he and his fellow impenitents were exiled to the most remote parts of the country. The Tain minister's place of banishment was Kintyre in Argyllshire, but before being sent there, he was imprisoned in the Castle of Doune in Perthshire. He escaped and found his way back to Tain, where he continued his preaching.

The King at length got to hear of this and in 1610 had his Privy Council send a sharp letter to the Provost and Magistrates of Tain upbraiding them on their iniquity in allowing "a person standing under his Majesty's offence to have so peaceable a residence as well as the free exercise of his calling among them", and ordering them to imprison John Munro. There is no record of John Munro's imprisonment, but some action by the Town Council had to be taken, and accordingly we find a new minister in Tain by 1612.

During the seventeenth century, the people of Easter Ross were caught up in the struggle between King and Covenant. David Ross, twelfth laird of Balnagown, and Chief of the Clan Ross, was one of the northern lairds who signed the National Covenant at Inverness in 1638, but after a time he forsook the Covenanting movement and became a Royalist. His conversion to the Royalist cause was, however, rather irresolute, for when the great Marquis of Montrose crossed from Orkney to Caithness in April 1650, Balnagown was once again with the Covenanting forces, mustering his Clan in readiness to oppose Montrose's passage to the south. In this he was probably influenced by his powerful neighbour, the Earl of Sutherland.

The Earl assembled a strong force to resist Montrose's advance, but when the Marquis entered Sutherland, he retired before him; but before doing so, he put strong garrisons in Skibo, Dunrobin, Skelbo and Dornoch. He also took the precaution of sending a strong escort with cattle and other goods to the hills, out of reach of the advancing enemy. The Earl then crossed the Meikle Ferry to Tain with three hundred men.

In the meantime, after some skirmishing, Montrose reached Strath Oykell with a force of only twelve hundred men. Here he halted for a few days in expectation of the arrival of the MacKenzies, and other reinforcements, whom he expected to join him. But time was running out for the great Marquis. The delay gave time for Lieutenant-Colonel Strachan to arrive at Tain with two hundred and thirty horsemen, where he was joined by a force of about five hundred men under the command of the Earl of Sutherland, Ross of Balnagown and Munro of Lemlair.

A council of war was held at Tain, and it was decided that the Earl of Sutherland and his men should return into Sutherland and attempt to get round the rear of Montrose's forces to intercept a possible retreat, while Strachan with his horse, supported by the Munros and Rosses, would make a direct attack.

As Strachan prepared to go forward, word was brought that Montrose had advanced to Carbisdale. This move brought the armies much nearer to each other, so it was decided to advance without delay.

Montrose's intelligence must have been poor, for

Strachan was able to advance within a mile and a half of him without being observed. He then concealed his men on the moor, which was covered with broom, and sent out a party of scouts under Captain Andrew Munro of Lemlair to reconnoitre. Munro returned with the information that Montrose was sending out a small reconnaisance force of about forty men, and on receiving this information, Strachan at once ordered a small body of his horses to move forward out of the broom and reveal their presence to the enemy, while the remainder of his force lay in hiding. The ruse was successful. Montrose's scouts returned to the main body and reported the presence of a mere handful of troops. This information put Montrose off his guard to such an extent that he was completely surprised at disadvantage on level ground near a pass called Invercharron, by the sudden appearance of Strachan's horsemen.

Montrose immediately attempted a strategic retreat with his infantry to a wood and craggy hill at a short distance in his rear, but he was quickly overtaken. His raw Orkney troops could make little resistance, and his foreign troops broke before the impetus of Strachan's horse and retired precipitately into the nearby woods, where they were pursued by the Munros and Rosses, who cut them down in great numbers. Two hundred of the fugitives were drowned while attempting to cross the river, and the rout became complete.

When he saw that the day was irretrievably lost, Montrose threw away his sword and his cloak, which was decorated with the star and garter, and made his escape by swimming the river. He made his way up Strath Oykell and for three days lay concealed in the hilly country around Assynt, but he was finally caught and made prisoner by Neil MacLeod of Assynt.

After the battle, Lieutenant-Colonel Strachan's troops and the Clansmen returned to Tain, bringing with them more than four hundred prisoners.

Some days later, the captive Marquis of Montrose was also taken across the Meikle Ferry, and lodged for a night at a house in Tain before he was taken south. His subsequent fate is well known.

In 1651, David Ross of Balnagown was again on the Royalist side; but this time on the side of a duly covenanted King, Charles II. As Chief of the Clan, he raised and fitted-out a regiment of Rosses at his own expense to help the King, and marched them over the border with the Scots army which met disastrous defeat at Worcester. During this engagement, many Easter Ross men were taken prisoner, and were sold as slaves to the American colonists. Ross of Balnagown was himself taken prisoner and lodged in the Tower. He died in 1653, and was buried in Westminster Abbey.

Some time after the Restoration in 1660 the King granted Balnagown's son David a pension of £200 a year in recognition of his father's loyal service.

David, the thirteenth laird of Balnagown, was very interested in architecture and during his lifetime, was responsible for a number of improvements and additions to his castle at Balnagown. He was also interested in building at Tain and during a period when he was Provost of Tain he was concerned with the rebuilding of the old Tolbooth or Tower.

The Tower, which was built in 1631, appears to have been in a rather dilapidated condition towards the latter part of that century, as we learn from the records that in 1661 it was seriously in need of repair, and that in 1665 the burgh "craved a grant for the repair of the steeple".

In 1666, David McCulloch, merchant of Tain, was accused of "doune casting of three bartisanes stones from the top of the stible (steeple)" to the danger of those below. David was obviously celebrating, as he was among other things, "accuseit for dameing at the provest" (a serious offence then) "all qch deed and crime the said David confessit". The significance of David's escapade lies in the fact that he was able to dislodge the stones from the turret, which suggests that the Tower was indeed in an unsafe condition.

In 1703, the inevitable happened and the old Tower, or part of it, was blown down during a violent storm. On the petition of the magistrates of Tain, the Privy Council ordained that a collection be made for the reconstruction of the building; and sufficient funds seem to have been forthcoming for the building to be started without delay, for in the year 1708 it was reported to the Convention of Royal Burghs that the Tower was nearing completion.

In that year David, thirteenth of Balnagown, was Provost, and as we have seen, had concerned himself with the rebuilding of the Tower; but unfortunately Stronach, the contractor, involved the Burgh in more cost than was "concerted", so that in spite of the optimistic report to the Convention, the work was by no means near completion, but had to be suspended for some years, and David of Balnagown did not live to see it completed.

In 1712, another attempt was made to complete the Tower, but financial difficulties slowed up the work; and there was a further delay when Stronach the builder left the site to work at repairing the Castle at Dornoch.

The Tower was at last completed in 1733, largely due to the financial help of another Provost of Tain, General Ross of Balnagown, who gifted the money to the magistrates to finish the work.

In spite of minor alterations during the last century, notably after a fire in 1832, the Tower remains substantially the same as shaped by Stronach. Pennant who saw it in 1769, described it as a large square tower decorated by five spires and Southey, the poet, who visited Tain fifty years later, records it as being old and "Flemish", having one large spire and four shorter ones at the corners. It is probable too, from earlier references to the repairing of the "steeple", that the present Tower bore some close resemblance to the original which had collapsed in the storm. Old masons' marks on the present Tower indicate that it may have been in part rebuilt from parts of the more ancient "steeple". High up on the conical part of the middle turret there is one stone, more weathered than those around it, on which is cut the following inscription: THIS WARK—BIGIT 1631 JHON MACKULLOCH BEING

PROVEST—and some feet below is another stone with the sole word BAILZIES inscribed. The rest is indecipherable, having apparently been chiselled away. The date on the stone is confirmed by an inscription on the large bell which hangs in the middle turret. This shows that the bell was cast by a Flemish master founder in 1630, and reads . . . ANNO. SOLI. GLORIA. MICHAEL. BVERGERHVYS. ME. FECIT (Glory be to God alone Michael Burgerhuis made me in the year 1630). This fine old bell still rings out, as it has done throughout the generations — on Sundays as church bell, and every evening at eight o'clock, as Curfew Bell — so perpetuating an ancient custom.

The Market Cross, which now stands restored, close within the shadow of the tower, was at one time situated some distance away, to the south side of the High Street. Its appearance then was rather different than today, the long column and lion being surrounded by a stone wall or building. This was literally the centre of the burgh; the scene of all civic functions; the place where proclamations were read out, and where royalty and the distinguished were received. On occasion too, it was the scene of public festivals and demonstrations.

One such took place in 1733, the year of the completion of the Tower. Then John MacRae, a burgess of Tain, to celebrate the return from abroad of his distinguished relative Captain MacRae, Governor of Madras, invited the magistrates of the burgh, and all the principal burgesses to broach a hogshead of wine at the Cross, and drink the healths of the King, Queen, Prince of Wales and the Royal Family, and those of Governor MacRrae and all his "fast friends". From there, we are told, the company "repaired to all the chief taverns of the town, where they repeated the aforesaid healths, and spent the evening with music and entertainments suitable to the occasion."

Celebrations of this kind were not infrequent during these days, and the eighteenth-century magistrates appear to have been the most convivial of beings, accepting every event within the burgh, however trivial, as an excuse for a "bumper"; and as events of national importance too, seldom passed unobserved, it is not surprising to find numerous entries for tavern and drink bills in the burgh account books of the period. These books record not only the social expenditure of the magistrates but the historic events of the day, as the following extract shows:

". . . 5th July, 1743. . . . A dozen sherry, peats for a bonfire, 22 pints of ale and 2 glasses at desire of Calrossy on receipt of ye news of ye battle of Dettingen. . . ."

In the same year we have the following entry:

"At entertaining David Munro ye Town's Agent, most of ye Counsell present, £28. 3s." From the expenditure point of view, at least, it would appear that in the Council's opinion, the latter event was as important as the celebration of Dettingen.

We find the Tain magistrates at their expansive best at the admitting of free burgesses; thus, in 1741: ". . . At making Lord Lovat's son, Mr. Joseph Munro and Inverchassley's children burgesses, £18. 18s."

There are many more such instances involving varying expenditure; but at the same time, the less exalted members of the community were not neglected. Fishermen, labourers and workmen all shared in the conviviality.

For example, in 1737 there is an entry: "Liquors with the fishers of Cullen, 18s." and later: "Paid Donald Munro for ale in his house, 18s."

It was apparently the custom to give men employed on burgh work a morning dram, and another to mark the completion of the work. During the rebuilding of the Tower, many a jorum must have passed round, and Stronach the contractor came in for his share, as we see by the following:

"1733. For Alexander Stronach's morning drink when he came in to see the Barticen (bartizan) head, 7/6d." "For 2 masons and pioners (labourers) morning drink when working at (do.) £1. 9. 6d."

This was at the time when the Tower was nearing completion, as the next entry indicates:

"To Stronach when he finished the Barticen, £3. 12s." Then, "To 2 pioners working at (do.) £1. 16s." Another item, probably connected work on the Tower, follows: ". . . mason for day in the quarries and morning drink, 15s."

In later entries, the reckoning is in Sterling, not in Scots. Dated 1762, this extract reads:

". . . at celebrating the King's coronation, £2. 4. 3d.", and later the same year ". . . at the Annual election of Magistrates, £6. 12. 11½d."; so that Sterling or not, the magistrates of that day deemed it appropriate to spend three times as much on toasting the health of the Council as on pledging His Majesty King George III.

It would appear, however, that Council expenditure depended more upon the congeniality of the company entertained than upon the nature and importance of the event; but even when the magisterial mood was one of gloom, the occasion called for a glass, as the following sombre entry shows: "July 15, 1741. . . . Drink to the guard at John Don's execution, £2. 12. 6d."

The Gallow hill, scene of this execution, is on Tain links, towards the west side, and is now surmounted by a flagstaff. The last public execution to be performed there took place in 1762, when a young mother, Katherine Ross, was condemned for the murder of her child. No local hangman, on this occasion, appears to have been available, or willing to carry out the execution, and the Inverness hangman was imported for the occasion. While the crowd, which had gathered to witness the carrying out of the law, was still gazing at the gibbet, a dove which had been circling overhead finally settled on the body, and this incident quite convinced the assembled people that she had been guiltless of the crime.

Apart from a few instances, such as those mentioned, the Tain hangman was happily seldom called upon to use his gibbet. Generally speaking, fewer crimes in Scotland carried the death penalty than in England; but nonetheless the local hangman found plenty of opportunity to practice his skill in other directions. In the seventeenth and early eighteenth centuries, his duties often involved the use of the branding iron and pincer. The "notour thief" got his nose pinched with irons, or his "lug nailed", and other offenders were branded, whipped, scourged, or put in the stocks or the jougs.

The hangman was a person of some civic importance, and was often rewarded with a handful of grain from every sack that came to market. The Tain hangman was granted a strip of land for cultivation. This piece of ground, still known today as the "Hangman's Rig", is located to the south side of the Kirksheaf road.

As the eighteenth century advanced, the office of hangman became increasingly unpopular, until by 1762, as we have seen, no one locally could be found willing to perform the duty; and as civilization and good taste progressed, such punishments as scourging and ducking lost favour, and eventually became obsolete.

By the middle of the century too, assaults by dagger or sword were becoming less rife. The Disarming Act of 1746 no doubt had some effect upon the changing situation; but an increasing respect for law and order was coming in, and even before the passing of this Act, the open carrying of weapons was becoming less fashionable, and instead of a sword the average laird or magistrate preferred to carry a riding crop or a cane.

Yet only a decade or two before duelling had been commonplace, and disputes, particularly those involving a point of honour, were customarily settled by the sword.

The last duel on record in Easter Ross took place in 1721. In June of that year, a magistrate of Tain, Bailie Hugh Ross, a son of Andrew Ross of Shand-

wick, after dining at Knockbreck with a neighbouring laird of the same name, Captain Hugh Ross of
Tolly, quarrelled violently with him. They adjourned
to a mound at Balkeith, afterwards known as the
Duel Hill, and fought a duel there without seconds.
The Bailie killed Ross of Tolly and fearing a trial
for murder, fled to Sweden. He is said to have fled
from the spot on horseback, and the supposed prints
of his horse's hooves on the moist ground were
carved out and preserved for many years. The
custom of carving out these prints did not survive
the nineteenth century, but the name of Duel Hill
has persisted, and is identified as the small sandhill
on the Fendom about a mile from Tain, close to the
water bridge.

Captain Hugh Ross of Tolly, the victim of the
duel, had been the officer chosen to lead the Easter
Ross loyalists during the rising of 1715.

The story of this rising and of that of 1745, as it
concerned Easter Ross, appears in the next chapter.

CHAPTER IV

THE UPRISINGS OF 1715 AND 1745

During the uprising of 1715, the men of Easter Ross appear to have been almost unanimously on the side of the government. Even a month before Mar raised his standard on 6th September, 1715, the Town Council of Tain "considering the Rumors and Confusione that is likely to happen through Britton, and ffinding their neighbours making motiones of reparatione for warre", were taking the precaution of appointing a nightly guard of ten men and a Captain to watch the town from 8.00 p.m. to 6.00 in the morning.

On 12th September, the Magistrates ordered all men between the ages of 16 and 60 to rendezvous on the links with "ther best cloaths and arms", and on the next day, on the High Street, so that they might receive their orders as to the defence of the town.

A few days later, fifty "sufficient fencible men" with four days' loaning (provision) were despatched under the command of Captain Hugh Ross of Tollie to join Captain Robert Munro of Foulis at Alness (this was the Hugh Ross who was killed in the duel at Balkeith, six years later).

All these preparations, however, did not prevent Lord Duffus, with the Earl of Seaforth in support, marching into Tain with between 400 and 500 men of the MacKenzies, Chisholms and MacDonalds, to proclaim James at the Market Cross. They then

Clan MacKenzie

Tain Courthouse and Council Chambers

hastened south to join the Earl of Mar.

The men of the Munros and Rosses, and others loyal to the Government, were in 1716 gathered at Fearn to the number of 700, ready to march to Inverness, but provisions were so scarce that the regiment was delayed, and was in fact disbanded soon afterwards, when the Chevalier returned to France in February, 1716.

After the uprising of 1715, the estates of some of the rebel Jacobite chiefs were declared forfeited and placed under Commissioners authorised to collect the rents for the Government; but the collection of these rents — particularly in the wilder and more inaccessible parts of the Highlands — was by no means an easy matter. The vast territory of the Earl of Seaforth in Ross-shire, which extended from Brahan castle to Kintail, and included the Isle of Lewis, presented a particular problem, for there was no approach to Lochalsh, Kintail and the remoter west except by narrow and difficult paths through bleak and hostile territory.

Seaforth, on his banishment in 1716, had entrusted the management of his forfeited estates to his factor Donald Murchison, and for several years the MacKenzie tenants flouted the Government by continuing to pay their rents to Murchison, who found means of sending them to the exiled Earl in France.

In 1720, the Commissioners at last found men courageous enough to attempt to collect the rents of the Seaforth property for the Government. These two men belonged to Tain — William Ross of Easter Fearn, an ex-provost of the burgh, and his brother Robert Ross, a bailie of Tain.

In February 1721, the brothers Ross sent messengers into the western districts, assuring the tenants of good usage if they would make peaceable submission, but these men were seized and robbed of their papers and arms. After further attempts at reasoning had produced no result, William and Robert Ross eventually set out on 13th September with a party of about 30 soldiers and a number of their own clansmen, determined to enforce the submission of the MacKenzie tenants; but Donald Murchison, who had collected about 350 men, all armed with firelocks, waited for them in the heights of Strathglass. As they pressed on, they were fired upon from a concealed height, and William Ross of Easter Fearn, riding ahead, was wounded in two places, but he still rode on as though unhurt, calling upon some of the Ross clansmen to go ahead of the soldiers and clear out those lurking in ambush. This the clansmen did, pretty effectively, and the whole party managed to advance about six miles until they came to a rocky pass, which unfortunately for them, was ideal for defence. Here Donald Murchison had forty men concealed in the heather who opened a deadly fire, inflicting a mortal wound on Walter Ross, Easter Fearn's son. Bailie Ross's son was also wounded by a bullet which passed across his chest. The bailie shouted to his son to retire, and although the order was obeyed, the two wounded youths and Bailie Ross's servant were taken prisoner and carried up a hill, where they were stripped of their clothes, arms, money and papers. Young Ross of Easter Fearn died next morning.

The invading party are said to have met the ambush with resolution, and even managed to drive out some of the opposing force from nearby places of concealment; but eventually finding that he was surrounded, Easter Fearn asked for a parley. He sent forward a messenger to ask who opposed the King's troops, and what were their demands. Murchison's men answered that first they must have Easter Fearn delivered up to them, but this was curtly refused. After some further talk, it was at length agreed that Ross of Easter Fearn should go forward to meet Donald Murchison. As Easter Fearn was in a hopeless position he had to agree to giving up his papers, and compacted under a penalty of £500 never again to officiate as a collector for the Government; after which he was given safe conduct to leave with his men.

In the "Forty-five" many of the northern clans remained loyal to the government. This was in no small measure due to the exertions of Lord President Duncan Forbes of Culloden, who by his undoubted influence, prevented a number of chiefs from joining Prince Charles Edward's banner. Forbes was related to the Rosses, both by blood and by marriage, and was confident of their support; but in this he was not entirely successful.

On the death in 1711 of David Ross of Balnagown, the last of the direct line of Balnagown, the Rosses of Pitcalnie were recognised by many as representing the family, though they did not succeed to the estates. Malcolm Ross, heir to Pitcalnie, and great-nephew of Lord President Forbes, in spite of family disapproval joined the Prince's army in October 1745, although only in the previous June he had been appointed to an ensigncy in Lord Loudoun's regiment. His conduct grieved and angered his relative, Duncan Forbes, who wrote an indignant letter to Pitcalnie on the 25th October.

"... I was never more astonished, and but seldom more afflicted in my life when I heard of the madness of your son. I cannot conceive by what magick he has been prevail'd on to forfeit utterly his own honour; in a signall manner to affront and dishonour me, whom you made answerable for him; to risk a halter, which, if he do not succeed, must be his doom, without any other tryall than that of a court martial ... the villians who seduced him ... I never will forgive, tho him I will if he return quickly to his duty. ..."

Lord President Forbes received twenty blank commissions from the War Office for the raising of companies of a hundred men from each of the "well affected" clans. A few clans quickly assembled, but at first there was considerable delay in raising the Rosses. Some attempt was made to gather them together, but young Pitcalnie's influence was such that many dispersed. Indeed, his "madness" for a time affected the whole clan, and there was such difficulty in gathering a sufficient number of Rosses to form a company that President Forbes, growing weary of the delay, addressed the following open letter to the clan.

Culloden House.
7th November, 1745.

"TO THE GENTLEMEN OF THE NAME OF ROSS.
Gentlemen,
    It is, I confess, a piece of presumption in me to address so many gentlemen, who each well deserved

a separate application, by one letter; but the hurry I am keept in is so great, and the occasion is so pressing that I hope you will forgive me. . . .

Upon the unexpected height to which the Rebellion now on foot blazed, his Majestie was pleased to trust me with the disposition of Commissions for raiseing som Independent Compys. amongst those kindred in the north whose disposition it was to support the Govt.; and it did not cost me one minute to resolve that no kindred could be better trusted than yours.

I acquainted Mr. Bailie, who has charge of the Master of Rosse's affaires, that the Master was to have one of the Compys. . . . to my great mortification I have been inform'd that the men who were assembled for that purpose were prevail'd upon to disperse, upon the interposition of ane unhappy youth, a near relation of mine. . . . What I therefore most earnestly entreat of you, whose affection to the Govt., as well as concern for the honour of the kindred, I am fully satisf'd of, is, that you should without loseing time, concert the proper measures for haveing this Compy. instantly made up of men, who shall not be understood to serve longer than till these troubles are over. . . ."

But the gentlemen of the name of Ross refused to be hurried. First of all there was business to be done at Tain and even though the fate of the Hanoverian dynasty might hang in the balance, for the time being at least, they felt the demands of commerce to be more pressing than a call to arms.

So, in a tactfully evasive letter, dated Tain, 10th November, 1745, the Gentlemen of Clan

Ross replied to the President:
"My Lord,

We had the honor of receiving your letter by our friend Captain Munro of Culcairn; and we beg leave to assure your Lordship of our attachement and regard to the present happy establishment. . . .

We have mett here this day in compliance with your letter; and as Captain Munro will deliver this, we doe referr him to acquaint your Lordship, at greater length than may be proper to write in a letter, what resolution we have come to, in order to make up the men expected from this country. But as there is a mercatt next week, at which all the people have necessary bussyness to doe, in order to enable them to pay their rents and other demands, wee are assured they will not willingly goe till that mercatt is over. But the week thereafter, we hope the men will be at Inverness. . . ."

Robert Ross, Simon Ross, Duncan Ross,
Thomas Ross, David Ross, David Ross,
Arthur Ross.

On the 15th November, Duncan Forbes wrote in some exasparation to one, George Ross, complaining about the Ross clansmen.

". . . Your namesakes have not, whether from knavery or folly, or a mixture of both, behaved themselves as I expected, or as they ought to have done. So soon as I received the commissions for the Independent compys., I sent for Mr. Baillie and Inverchassly, and acquainted them with my intention of giveing one to the Master of Ross, with the Lieut and Ensign that were proposed. They seem'd well satisfyd, found no difficulty in raiseing the compy., and promised to bring the men together as soon as they should have notice; which could not be sooner than when we could have arms and money; when they came, they had notice and brought 100 men together; but upon some difficultys raised by Pitcalny's mad son, they dispers'd; and tho' I have wrote them as a kindred, a letter, and sent Culcairn to Tain, where he had meetings with them, all I have got from them is a promise that in a fortnight the compy. will be brought together. I do not choose to conjecture at the cause of the backwardness in the people; it is surely not disaffection. . . ."

This recalcitrance on the part of the Rosses was particularly exasperating to Duncan Forbes as his recruiting in Ross had already suffered a set back by the action of the Earl of Cromartie and his son, Lord MacLeod, who had not only spurned a commission, but had marched off to join the Prince with 400 men.

On the other hand, he was cheered by the fact that the Munros, close neighbours and friends of the Rosses, had raised a company under the captaincy of George Munro of Culcairn, without much difficulty, and Hugh MacLeod of Geanies had mustered another hundred men from Assynt.

It now remained for the Rosses to join the faithful; and although the President could not readily doubt "the kindred", their delaying tactics were giving him anxious moments. To add to his disquiet, intelligence reports from the neighbourhood had not been too reassuring. David Rose of Tarlogie had written to him hinting of a lack of enthusiasm for King George in certain quarters, " .. . Severalls I never suspected," he wrote, "are to say no worse, very cool. . . ."

The Rosses were in fact divided. Some were openly in sympathy with young Ross of Pitcalnie, and others, who might perhaps favour the government, hesitated to take up arms against their friends. Much depended upon the Master of Ross who was absent in London. He, the President believed, would have the necessary influence to prod on at least his Balnagown tenants, and his recall was now essential. But communications were slow, and it was 14th December before the Master of Ross returned. He made the journey north by sea, accompanied significantly enough, by John Forbes, the President's son. His ship, the Hound sloop of war, was carrying much needed arms — a fact that may have had some stimulus on recruiting — for within a fortnight or so, a Ross Independent Company was at last raised under his command.

The Ross Company was ordered to march to Inverness, and arrived there on 6th January, 1746 — not surprisingly, the last of the Independent Companies to get there — a distinction narrowly won from a party of MacKays who had entered the town only two days previously.

Inverness was by this time a garrison town; but when Lord Loudoun, Commander in Chief of the King's forces in the north, had arrived there in October, his command was at first a mere 150 men, most of them from his own regiment; but before the end of the month he was joined by George Munro of Culcairn with his Company of Munros, and a Sutherland Company led by Alexander Gunn. The

Grants were next to arrive and at intervals, as they were raised, other Companies followed, until by the end of the year an irregular force of nearly 2,000 was assembled at Inverness.

The arrival of the Ross and MacKay contingents in January was a welcome addition to this strength; but even with these reinforcements Lord Loudoun's force was greatly inferior in numbers to the Jacobite army now making its way north.

When reports arrived on 18th February that the Prince's army was rapidly approaching Inverness, Loudoun outnumbered, and believing his position to be untenable, promptly prepared to abandon the town. Leaving the Rosses and the Grants, with 80 regular soldiers to garrison the castle of Inverness, he retreated across the Firth by way of Kessock Ferry. By retiring northwards, his lordship hoped not only to save his army, but to draw off as many of the Prince's force as possible in pursuit.

In this, at least, he was successful, for when Charles entered Inverness later in the day, he immediately sent a strong detachment of picked troops in chase of Loudoun. The Prince then directed his attention to the Castle. Grant of Rothiemurchus, who was governor, received a summons to surrender, which he refused, so at once the siege began. Engineers of the Prince's army proceeded to undermine the castle and plant explosives beneath. The Rosses and Grants within the castle walls remained defiant for two days, but on the 20th February when the mining was complete, and the fortress was in danger of blowing up, the garrison surrendered. After the surrender, the castle was blown up by order of the Prince.

When Lord Loudoun retreated northwards from Inverness, Lord President Duncan Forbes went with him. On 21st February they were at Balnagown, and here they took up positions against the advancing enemy; but on the following day intelligence was received that the rebel force was approaching in such force that both Lord Loudoun and the President thought it advisable to leave Balnagown for Tain and then retreat across the Dornoch Firth, by way of Meikle Ferry, into Sutherland. In anticipation of such a move they had previously arranged with the Earl of Sutherland to get all the available boats from Sutherland to the Ferry at Tain; and by means of these and all the boats that could be gathered together on the Tain side of the Firth, their troops were quickly transported across the Firth on Sunday, 23rd February.

The crossing was so smoothly and rapidly carried out that the pursuing army were completely unaware of the manoeuvre. The Earl of Cromartie, who was in command, had halted awhile at Dingwall and taken the opportunity of visiting his home at Brahan. When he resumed his march towards Tain, and had reached Alness bridge, information reached him that Lord Loudoun had crossed the Firth some two days before. Cromartie and his men then decided to return temporarily to Dingwall, which was a day's march from both Inverness and Tain; but about a fortnight later they were in Tain in great numbers, now accompanied by the Duke of Perth, who had charge of operations. They made Tain their headquarters, and during their stay there,

made every possible effort to obtain money, provisions, meal and other necessities from the burgh
and the surrounding district. Sixty pounds sterling
was exacted from Tain alone — a considerable
amount of wealth at that time — and about half
the burgh's revenue.

Lord Loudoun's headquarters were at Dornoch.
His regiment was billeted there and in the nearby
farm houses, and the rest of the companies were
spread westward across country, guarding all the
main passes and fords to the north.

The two armies lay opposite each other, the
waters of the Firth between, until Thursday, 20th
March. On that day, a thick fog hung over the
Dornoch Firth, and under cover of this, a strong
force of the rebels, who had secretly collected
together a number of fishing boats from Findhorn,
and other places on the Moray coast, sailed them
round Tarbat Ness, crossed the Meikle Ferry unobserved, and took Loudoun's men completely by
surprise. So unexpected was the landing that, on the
way to Dornoch, the assault force overtook and
dispersed about 200 of Loudoun's regiment before
they could put up any effective resistance. Their
commander, Major MacKenzie was captured along
with several other officers and about 60 men. Some
who escaped joined the main body of Lord
Loudoun's troops, who, on receiving the alarm were
making their way westwards. They were pursued by
the rebel army as far as the head of Loch Shin, but
here the chase was given up.

Lord Loudoun, accompanied by President Forbes
and some of the scattered Companies, eventually

escaped to Skye. Lord MacLeod, son of the Earl of
Cromartie, who was with the attaching force, wrote
an account of the affair, from which the following
extract is taken: ". . . in the morning we gote an
express from Tain to acquaint us that several large
boats were arriv'd there from the coast of Murray.
We immediately went into the town. These boats
having been sent by the Prince's orders for trans-
porting of the troops at Tain into Sutherland, the
enemy having carried away or destroy'd all the
boats thereabouts. Everything having being gote
ready that day and the following night, the first
division of our troops cross'd over into Sutherland
next morning led by the Duke of Perth, and landed
without opposition, being unobserv'd by the enemy
by reason of a thick fog. As we were to cross over at
different times, by reason that our boats were too
few, and as my father's regiment was to be in the
last division, I cross'd with the Frasers expecting
that there would be some action at which I was
desirous of being present. But the enemy as soon as
they discovered our being landed retir'd. The county
militia went to their respective homes, and the Earl
of Sutherland cross'd over the Firth of Murray to
the Duke of Cumberland's army. The Earl of
Loudoun and President Forbes retir'd with Sir
Alexander MacDonald and the Laird of MacLeod
and their men into the Isle of Sky. The greater
part of Lord Loudoun's regiment was made
prisoner of war, together with their Major, William
MacKenzie. . . ."

The Independent companies, as Lord MacLeod's
account suggests, were more or less completely

broken up by the Jacobite surprise attack. The
MacKays returned to the north, the Sutherlands
resorted to their local hill country, and the
MacLeod, MacDonald and Munro companies with-
drew to Skye with Loudoun and the President. The
Duke of Perth then returned with most of the
insurgent troops to Inverness, leaving the Earl of
Cromartie with a well-armed force to keep an eye
on any loyalist remnants left in Sutherland.

Part of this force, under the command of Lord
MacLeod, scoured Caithness in an attempt to
raise supplies and recruits, while the Earl of
Cromartie remained at Dunrobin, which he had
made his headquarters; but on receiving a message
from the Prince that his men were urgently needed
at Inverness to strengthen the Jacobite army there,
the Earl hastily recalled his scattered forces, and
proceeded to march south from Dunrobin.

He had only marched a few miles from Golspie
when he was attacked by a band of loyalists commanded by Ensign MacKay. MacKay's men, who
had been hiding in the hills, and had been secretly
receiving supplies of ammunition, attacked so
suddenly that Cromartie's small army, taken un-
awares, was quickly driven towards the Little Ferry.
There they made a stand, but were in the end
defeated, and many of them were drowned in
attempting to escape across the Ferry.

The day after this engagement the battle of
Culloden was fought, and it may well be that the loss
of his reinforcements from the north contributed in
some measure to Prince Charles Edward's final
defeat.

CHAPTER V

TAIN — DINGWALL—
AN OLD CONTROVERSY

The occupation of Tain by the Prince's army in the Spring of 1746 caused the burgh a great deal of hardship. The rebel army, it will be recalled, more or less sacked the town and made ". . . arbitrary demands for cess, levie money and loan from the burgh under pain of military execution, and that notwithstanding the magistrats have plead poverty. . . ."

Yet within two years of the Jacobite troubles a remarkable economic improvement had taken place, largely due to the introduction of the linen industry to Tain.

Between 1747 and 1748 the British Linen Company sent three spinning mistresses and a master heckler by ship from Leith to Tain, to instruct the inhabitants in the art of weaving. Some weaving had, in fact, been carried on in the Tain district for some years before the British Linen Company's venture, but the Company succeeded in establishing the industry on a sound commercial footing, giving much needed local employment.

Even so, it would seem that all available local labour was not absorbed, for in 1750, when the Company's interests were expanding, there was apparently no great difficulty in finding extra labour. In that year, John Reid "Merchant in

Tayne", who was also the British Linen Company's manager there, petitioned the Council for a piece of land "closs to the Washing Burn" to "carry on weaving . . . to keep in employment numbers of Idlers and people. . . ."

Much of the British Linen Company's business was carried by sea to Tain and Cromarty, and the appearance of extra shipping in these waters was of great advantage to local merchants and trades-people by keeping them in touch with the capital and the commercial south.

A Stent Roll of Tain, dated 1756, gives some idea of the diversity and the number of the trades carried on in the burgh at that time. Included in the roll are 21 weavers, 23 merchants, 3 masons, 8 wrights, 4 coopers, 3 musicians — one of them being a glover as well — 2 more glovers, 3 wigmakers, 10 tailors, 29 shoe-makers, 4 millers, 1 thatcher, 8 smiths (including a silversmith, a gunsmith and a pewterer), 3 brewers, 3 chapmen, 2 dyers and 7 boat-men. To this rather impressive list should be added 1 writer, or lawyer, 1 surgeon and at least 2 school teachers.

The eighteenth-century magistrates appear on the whole to have taken a rather progressive view of schooling and education, and the burgh treasurers' reports show that a proportion of the town's income was spent on salaries for the school masters and mistresses. These salaries were by no means munificent, as the following extracts for 1766 to 1768 show: "David Munro schoolmaster 1766 and 1767, £5. Mr. Cameron schoolmaster 1767 and 1768, £22. 4. 5. David Munro salary 1768, £2. 10. 0.

Paid the Miss's Luttit schoolmistress, £3. Paid Miss Ann Luttit schoolmistress, £7. . . ." These sums were in sterling. In 1752, Mr. Samuel Paply master of the grammar school at Tain received £100 Scots (equal to about £8. 6. 8 sterling).

In the middle of the eighteenth century there were apparently two schools in Tain. One of them, the Grammar School — which was then situated somewhere off Tower Street, within the corner of what is now the old cemetery — had been in existence from the middle of the sixteenth century, or even earlier. From the burgh account books we learn that the school house had two storeys, and that the headmaster and his wife rented the upper rooms. Both the headmaster and his wife appear to have taught at the school, but the accounts of 1774 indicate that by then the school had two masters and a mistress.

Medicine seems to have been practised in Tain in the seventeenth century, but records for this period are scanty. We hear of Thomas Ross, chirurgeon (surgeon) in Tain in 1687 — a remote and shadowy figure who used fearsome instruments such as "sheirs" and "ane yron botikin" — but the later and more complete records give us a more intimate and revealing glimpse of the character and work of doctors who practised in Tain during the eighteenth century.

The resident doctor in Tain about the year 1717 was Dr. Alexander Ross. He was by all accounts an extremely colourful character, and is said to have been "a good sportsman, a good scholar, and a popular physician"; but he was also a great lover of argument, particularly on his favourite subjects,

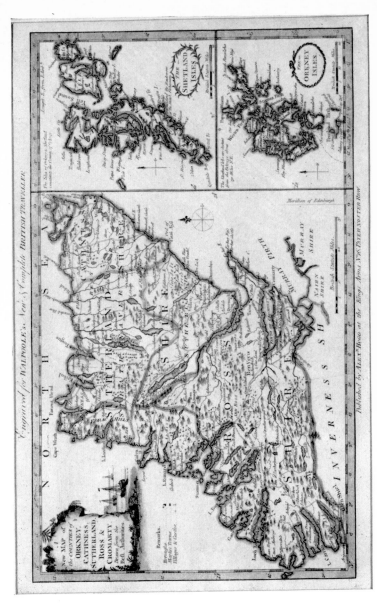

Engraved by *Thomas Conder*, 1780

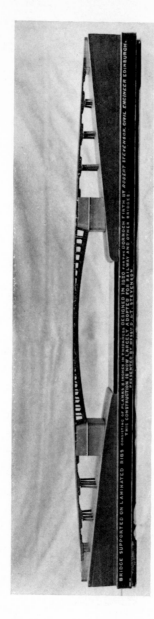

BRIDGE SUPPORTED ON LAMINATED RIBS CONSISTING OF PLANKS 18 INCHES IN THICKNESS DESIGNED IN 1830 FOR THE DORNOCH FIRTH BY ROBERT STEVENSON, CIVIL ENGINEER EDINBURGH. THIS CONSTRUCTION IS NOW LARGELY ADOPTED FOR RAILWAY AND OTHER BRIDGES. MODEL PRESENTED BY MESSRS D.& T. STEVENSON.

Laminated wooden girder bridge designed in 1830 by Robert Stevenson (of Bell Rock Lighthouse fame) for spanning the Dornoch Firth.

The bridge was never built but the model remains and is used in the museum to demonstrate the type of bridge where by laminar construction an arch can be made in excess of the maximum length of timber available.

metaphysics and theology. His enthusiasm for debate at length landed him in serious trouble with the Church Presbytery. The Presbytery tried him and he was found guilty of profaning the Lord's day by habitually absenting himself from church ordin-ances, and also of heresy by arguing and talking of the Scriptures "as though they were but a tradition".

He was sentenced to stand in sackcloth before the congregation of Tain on specified Sundays and make a full confession of his faith; but the wily doctor was unperturbed. He obediently turned up at the church door on the appointed days, but always at the crucial moment, when about to undergo the penalty for his transgressions, his servant Rory Roy, on the doctor's secret instructions, made a sudden appearance in a great hurry and gasped out "Lady Clyne has broke her leg and wants the dochter aawful bad" or, on another occasion — "Donald Ross, Edderton is very baad, bewitched or poisoned, and wants the dochter" or again, "David Munro, Tarbat has fallen out of his boat and is drowned and wants the dochter!"

This little comedy was played for some consider-able time and, with the assistance of the faithful Rory Roy, the doctor managed to avoid his due punishment on each and every occasion he was called upon to appear at the church; but at last he grew tired of the act and left Tain to take up practice at Dornoch.

In 1735 there was a doctor John McKilligan in Tain, who was something of a "fashionable doctor". The following copy of an account for medicines supplied to one of his richer clients throws an interesting light on the pharmacy of his day:

"Dr. to Jn. McKilligan Surgeon in Tayne, December 20th, 1735.

Janrie	3.	To prepard crabs eyes for your child	10
		To a box of pills for the toothack for your lady	2:10
Janrie	10.	To a burgundy pitchplaister	2
		To an emollient electuary	10
Febrie	4.	To discuping ointment	1:2
Febrie	6.	To a vomit	1:0
		To blooding	1:0
Febrie	14.	To seven drops purging pills	7:0
		To twenty doses antihysterick pills	16:0
		To mololot plaister	6
Spt.	2.	To a vomit	1:0
Dec.	13.	To four doses doobstruent pills	4:0
		To blooding Mrs. Bell	1:6
Dec.	14.	To a mixture for the ears	2:4
		To a years sallary due Marts	£1:1:0

Arbol the 22nd of March 1737."

Tain seems to have been without a doctor for a few years, dating from about 1740, for a Town Council Minute of 1744 states: "Town . . . for some years past destitute of any surgeon, nay, any capable blood persons in sickness, and that there is a young man of that business lately come to town . . . and town's revenue in Common Good is at present providentially encreased . . . agree to pay Hugh Mcffarqr, surgeon, fifty merks yearly for his encouragement to reside in the burgh . . . during their pleasure, provided always he keep a reasonable stock of druggs for the use of town and country, and behaves himself in his station and profession as becometh, and which summ is given him as assistance to fforme a House and Garden . . . in which garden he is required to keep Herbs necessary for his profession. . . ."

Dr. McFarquhar remained in Tain for about fifty years, during which time he became a respected member of the community, a member of the town council and eventually senior Bailie of the burgh.

We have also a record of some of the drugs prescribed by the worthy doctor during his long years of practice. Among these may be mentioned at random "strenthening plaister — oyl of whyte lilies — cordial julep — syrup of whyte poppies — ipecan tincture—tincture of rhubarb—cammail flowers—oyl of mace — sacred tincture—tincture of caster — spirement water — and snake root." Some of these remedies have only gone out of favour in recent years.

A number of recipes, much in vogue in Doctor MacFarquhar's day, and later, were made basically of whisky. One, a popular stomach cordial, was made with whisky and added carminatives such as cloves, coriander and cinnamon. Another, used as a remedy for chills, was simply whisky with added hot water and cinnamon. This is not without its advocates today.

Whisky was distilled in many of the small farms and crofts in Easter Ross and in the Highlands generally, as an important adjunct to farming. The draff, or residue of the barley left after distillation, was used to feed the animals and the straw was also used for feeding in winter, while the whisky itself was quickly converted into cash to help to meet the rent.

Brewing of ale was also carried out in the crofts and homes in the north, and ale rather than whisky was the common man's drink. As it was sold in the tavern at the relatively cheap price of 2d. a Scotch pint — which was equal to two English pints — it was within the reach of most.

It is little wonder then, that when Parliament decided to impose the same malt duties in Scotland as those already current in England, many Highlanders regarded this as an unwarranted interference with their native rights and liberties and, in defiance of all the edicts, carried on brewing and distilling illegally.

A document dated 1742 lists the names of 11 Tain people who had contravened the law by "brewing ale without notice", and "malting without notice". In the same year there were charges against another 31 people in Tain for illicit brewing in such places as a garret, a byre, a loft and a cellar; and in 1746, there were charges against no fewer than 50 people in Tarlogie, Rhynie, Pitkerrie, Pitcalnie, Nigg and Cadboll for "brewing in secret places without entry".

An extract from a complaint to the baron bailie of Balnagown reads: "Notwithstanding that orders were issued to suppress . . . from brewing and selling ale and aqua vitae (whisky) . . . still persist . . . these little by-brewers are so much haunted (have so many customers) that complainers can make little of it. . . ."

Magistrates found the greatest difficulty in enforcing the law as the brewing of ale had for so long been an accepted part of the domestic life and work. In the eighteenth century, as we have seen, it was the custom to give ale or "drink-money" to everyone who performed a task or a service, be it digging a ditch, delivering a load of peats or running an errand; and this convivial habit persisted in spite of taxation.

Apart from ale and spirits, claret was the universally popular drink, and up to 1780 it was imported from France duty free and sold so cheaply that it was to be found in almost every home. Some of the finer vintages appeared on the tables of the merchants and land owners, many of whom were very hearty claret drinkers; but from all accounts, probably few could equal the prowess of two Easter Ross Lairds — Ross clansmen both — whose capacity for wine appears to have been rather phenomenal, even by eighteenth century standards.

One, Alexander Ross, first of Ankerville, probably served his apprenticeship among the wine devotees of Easter Ross, but he gained his laurels abroad. He went into the service of Augustus, King of Poland, and "being the only person who could bear more liquor than his Majesty he got to be a Commissary. . . ." On return to his native country he purchased the estate of Ankerville, Nigg, where, according to Bishop Pococke, "he built and lived too greatly for it, was for determining all things by the Sabre; and died much reduced in his finances. . . ."

The other was David Ross of Inverchassley, better

known as Lord Ankerville, one of the senators of the college of Justice. Born in 1727, he studied law, and was admitted to the bar in 1751. He sat on the bench for 29 years, but in spite of a busy legal life, which demanded much of his time in Edinburgh, he managed to devote a great deal of his attention to the affairs of Tain, and at one time was Provost of the Royal Burgh.

In *Kay's Edinburgh Portraits* he is described as having an "unswerving devotion to the pleasures of the table", and in particular, that "he preferred claret to any other species of wine". "Every year," says his biographer, "Lord Ankerville travelled north to his seat of Tarlogie, near Tain in Ross-shire.... This long journey he performed in leisurely manner, by short and easy stages; and, as he dined and slept all night at the end of each, his hosts of the Highland road were careful always to have a select potion of their best claret set aside for their guest.... The annual migration from north to south, and from south to north became a matter of as nice regularity as the cuckoo's song in Spring; and as well did the Highland innkeeper at half-a-mile's distance, know the rumbling, creaking chaise of the one, as he did the monotonous tone of the other.

The quantity of claret drank by his Lordship on these annual journeys has been variously estimated and, although no satisfactory statement has been given, all agree that it must have been immense."

The old Judge's love of claret did not abate with his increase of years and apparently it impaired neither his constitution nor his reputation, for he died in 1805 at the venerable age of 78, esteemed and respected by all. Ankerville Street in Tain perpetuates his memory.

Another well-known eighteenth-century legal character who belonged to Easter Ross, and who also had the honour of having a Tain street named after him was Sheriff Donald MacLeod of Geanies, and the street today bears the name of Geanies Street.

Before Geanies Street was made, the main entrance from the south to the High Street in Tain, was by way of King Street. About 20 to 30 yards east of King Street there was a broad, deep hollow through which a swiftly flowing burn, known as the *Ault-maitach*, ran to the sea. This was then the eastern boundary of the burgh, and beyond this were open fields and gardens with some scattered buildings; but in 1789, Sheriff MacLeod, who owned property and land in this area, offered the Tain Town Council the "liberty of opening a new communication twixt the Town and the County, Eastward and Southward of it by a street or road to be carried from Knockbreck Road through the field now occupied by Dr. McFarquhar, until it gets to the line of the High Street. . . ."

Sheriff MacLeod made it a condition of his offer that the town should contribute to the expense of building a bridge over the *Ault-maitach* to complete the way to the High Street, and the Town Council considering that the suggested new route was "a more easy and agreeable access to the town", agreed to the plan; so Geanies Street was built — a wide and spacious street — and a credit to Sheriff MacLeod and the planners of his day.

Donald MacLeod of Geanies was appointed Sheriff of Ross in 1774, and he served in this capacity for the very long period of 59 years. As Sheriff he had the power to convene the County meetings, and of fixing the place of meeting, at Tain or Dingwall, whichever he thought fit; but during his long term of office he chose to hold the meetings, almost without exception, at Tain.

His unalterable and unvarying choice of Tain for so many years was resented, and sometimes resisted, by the people of Wester Ross, who claimed Dingwall to be more central and convenient.

There had long been dissension between Easter and Wester Ross as to which Royal Burgh should have precedence in the affairs of the County, and on occasion, this had even been the subject of litigation. The underlying cause of friction may perhaps date back as far as 1503, when Parliament constituted the Sheriffdoms of Ross and Caithness. In the Act it was stated, *inter alia*, ". . . that there be one Sheriff made of Ross which shall have full power and jurisdiction and Sheriffdom within the bounds of Ross, and to sit and have his place for Administration of Justice in Tain or Dingwall, as the Sheriff thinks expedient, for the decision of cases, briefs, or any other such things belonging to his office as the case requires. . . ."

It is noted that the Act of 1503 did not give one burgh precedence over the other, and a later Act of Parliament in the year of Charles II, dated 1661, and entitled "An Act anent the division of Ross from Inverness", did not make the matter any clearer, for in the original phrasing of this document, the name of the burgh which was to be the centre of "all legal exaction" was, for some unexplained reason, omitted. As a consequence, there was a great deal of wrangling throughout the years between Easter and Wester Ross, and in particular, between the Royal Burghs of Tain and Dingwall, for each claimed to be the Head Burgh.

In 1773, the dispute was taken to the Court of Session, where after due deliberation Lords Braxfield and Covington decided the case in favour of Tain.

No one, it may be certain, approved more of their Lordships' decision than Donald MacLeod of Geanies, who was appointed Sheriff of Ross in the following year, and thenceforth was to prove himself a strong and uncompromising supporter of the claims of Tain. He held the County meetings exclusively at Tain despite mutterings of dissent from the West: and so the squabbling went on until a great row erupted over a meeting at Tain in the year 1782.

Representatives from Dingwall at this meeting put forward a resolution that the next meeting be held at Dingwall. The motion was unexpectedly carried, and immediately afterwards the Sheriff Clerk principal hastily gathered up the minute books and other records within his reach and carried them away with him to Dingwall.

Sheriff MacLeod and the men of Tain were loud in proclaiming that both the vote and the Sheriff Clerk's action were highly irregular and downright illegal.

Once more the controversy was taken to the

Court of Session, and once more the judges found in favour of Tain. An appeal was, however, made to the House of Lords in 1784, and this time the Lords upheld the Court's decision that the vote and the Sheriff Clerk's conduct were illegal, but they did not support the judgment that Tain was Head Burgh. Thus, the real issue remained unresolved, and it was not until 1843 that the answer was found.

In that year, a Bill declaring Dingwall Head Burgh was pressed through the House of Commons. In August of the same year it was approved by the House of Lords and received the Royal assent and so the age-old dispute was at last brought to an end.

CHAPTER VI

THE MEIKLE FERRY DISASTER

As the eighteenth century advanced, new methods of farming began to be adopted in many parts of Scotland, but these were slow to spread north; and even towards the end of the century, in the comparatively fertile and extensively cultivated district of Easter Ross, there was a reluctance to change from the ancient ways.

In an old *Statistical Account* we learn that about 1792, with few exceptions, the old Scots plough was in use in the smaller farms and crofts in the parish of Fearn, and that this was pulled either by six or eight oxen, or by four oxen and two horses; and at the same period, farmers in the parish of Tarbat used ploughs drawn by six to eight oxen, or sometimes, two oxen and two horses.

In the same *Account*, the Rev. Alexander MacAdam, writing of the parish of Nigg, records: "The farmers keep a great stock of black cattle, which they employ in tilling their grounds" . . . "but," he adds prophetically, "it is supposed they shall soon be obliged to adopt a different method, because a great part of the Highlands, where their cattle were wont to be grazed in the summer season, are now converted into sheep-farms, the number of which is still increasing."

The Rev. MacAdam's fears were well founded, for in Easter Ross and elsewhere in the northern

Highlands, during his day, small crofts were being absorbed into bigger holdings, and then let to sheep farmers from the south of Scotland and the borders, who could afford much larger rents than the small crofter tenants.

Sir John Ross, the laird of Balnagown, was one of the first of the local land owners to interest himself in the new sheep farming methods, and in 1781 he offered a farm for the raising of sheep, to a sheep farmer from the south, by name Geddes. This move was feared and resented by the small tenant-farmers, of Easter Ross, for to most of them it presaged the eventual loss of their own small acres, and so they gave the incoming farmer all the trouble and annoyance that they could.

Despite this, and the fact that 1782 and 1783 were years of crop failure, famine and hardship, Geddes and his sheep remained and prospered. The point was not lost on other landlords and sheep runs gradually spread over Easter Ross and the north.

At length, in the Autumn of 1792, the cottar people of the hill districts, despairing and desperate, decided to drive the hated sheep out of the County. They assembled at Lairg and from there drove all the sheep they could gather on the way, through Lairg, Creich and Kincardine, onwards across the Struie, until in four days they had thousands of sheep driven across country as far as Alness.

But by this time the landlords and great stock farmers had furiously invoked the power of the law, and Sheriff Donald MacLeod of Geanies, as though he were dealing with a full scale rebellion, called in the military to assist. Troops of the 42nd regiment were ordered to proceed, by forced marches and by the shortest routes, to Easter Ross; but when they reached Alness, there were no enemy, for the people, warned of their coming, had quietly dispersed.

Eighteen of the drovers were, however, caught and sent to Inverness for trial. According to General Stewart in *Sketches of the Highlanders*, "They were eloquently defended by Mr. Charles Ross, advocate, one of their own countrymen; but as their conduct was illegal, and the offence clearly proved, they were found guilty and condemned to be transported to Botany Bay." The prisoners somehow managed to make their escape, and General Stewart comments that ". . . though the legality of the verdict and sentence could not be questioned, these did not carry along with them the public opinion, which was probably the cause that the escape of the prisoners was in a manner connived at; for they disappeared out of prison, no one knew how, and were never inquired after or molested."

It was said at the time that the great sheep drive caused "little less alarm among some of the gentlemen of Ross than the Rebellion of 1745"; but it was the men who drove the sheep that had real cause for alarm. They were, for the most part, poor crofters who saw their livelihood threatened by the intruding sheep; and, as to their conduct, General Stewart observed that ". . . no act of violence or outrage occurred, nor did the sheep suffer in the smallest degree beyond what resulted from the fatigue of the journey and the temporary loss of their pasture." Stewart also pointed out that the drovers "though pressed with hunger, did not take a single animal for their own use."

It would be true to say that the crofters from the hills and straths of Easter Ross suffered more from the invading sheep than those of the low lying and more arable lands; for in the cultivated areas, where much of the earth was turned over by the plough, space was limited for sheep raising. In addition, agriculture provided more employment than sheep grazing, and the lot of the agricultural worker was steadily improving during the eighteenth century. As the century progressed, wages increased, and by 1796, a ploughman's wages were about three times as much as they had been about thirty years before.

Prices also tended to rise and the *Old Statistical Account* informs us that they had roughly doubled within twenty years; yet about the year 1792, butcher meat in Easter Ross was only 2d. to 3d. a pound; hens and ducks were 3d. to 6d. each, and eggs were 8, 10 or 12 for 1d., according to season.

These prices seem very reasonable by present-day standards, but when related to the purchasing power of their day, there is no real comparison.

In the late eighteenth century money was by no means plentiful, and rents were often paid in produce, with the result that the economy tended to fluctuate with the seasons. A bad year often brought ruin and starvation with it, as happened in 1783, when the crops were a failure all over the Highlands. There was a desperate shortage of food, and the people of Easter Ross were faced with famine. In March of that year, the Town Council of Tain held a special meeting to consider ". . . the distressed and calamitous situation of the poor inhabitants of the town . . ." and directed that "... . the sum of £10 stg. shou'd be given out of the Town's ffunds to be added to the voluntary contributions of the other Gentlemen and Inhabitants of the place, in order to be laid out in the purchase of meal or barley to be distributed among the poor Inhabitants in quantities according to their different necessaties. . . ."

In December of the same year, a meeting of the land owners and their factors took place in Tain, under the chairmanship of Sheriff Donald MacLeod of Geanies "in order to take into consideration the state of the tenantry . . . and to form some plan whereby they might convey some effectual relief to their distressed situation". The meeting was "unanimously of the opinion that the situation of the whole of this country is extremely critical, and that if severe and harsh means are adopted by the proprietors of Estates in forcing arrears of payment at this time, though the conversion should be at a low rate, it must have the effect of driving the tenantry into despondency, and bringing the great majority of them into immediate and inevitable ruin; and in doing so will go near to lay the country waste ... and if once the present tenantry are removed, there will be very little probability of getting them replaced from any other country."

The years 1782 and 1783 were, however, years of great hardship not only for the tenantry, but for many of the lairds and small proprietors, and some idea of their circumstances may be gathered from letters of the period.

Simon Ross of Gledfield wrote to David Ross, Lord Ankerville's factor, at the time, complaining that he had no feeding for his cattle and that the last stack of corn intended for seed oats was done, as he had given the animals "the corn and straw as it grew". "They must perish," he wrote, "if I cannot get hay from Lord Ankerville . . . . an ounce can not be got anywhere else. . . . We have a fresh storm every day, the heather is so covered. . . . I believe all the cattle in our county will be lost."

William Ross of Gruinyairds also wrote to the factor, in great distress, "The crops was neither fit for meal or seed, being damnifyed with the heavy storms before it was gathered. . . . I know not which hand to turn to."

During these lean years, however, there was some relief. Sir John Ross of Balnagown, from his estates in the south, sent meal and seed to his tenants, and a number of other landlords aided with seed or produce. The government shipped 300 bolls of victual to be distributed free among the poor of the various parishes, and a further 300 bolls to be sold at a cheap rate. In addition, the contributor to the *Statistical Account* of the parish of Fearn informs us that "Providence was kind in these days of scarcity, in providing fish from the sea, so that not only the ordinary fisherman caught abundance, and sold them to the poor until the crop grew up, but many people joined, got different cobles and caught a quantity of cuddies, red codlings and flounders near the shore; also a quantity of fine cockles were had near Tain."

The fact that the latter were gathered on one of

the sand banks in the Dornoch Firth, known as the Mussel Scalps, where in previous years only mussels were to be found, was regarded as something of a miracle. The writer of the Tain section of the *Statistical Account* observed — "It is remarkable though cockles be not usually found on this bank, that in 1783, when there was a great scarcity of bread, it afforded in April, May and June, immense quantities of them, of an excellent quality, which contributed to the support of multitudes, not only in the parish, but in the neighbourhood."

In a part of the country where meal was the staple food, and where there was complete dependence on locally grown crops, there was always a seasonal risk of scarcity; but in the two decades following the bad years of 1782 and 1783, there was no serious shortage of food in Easter Ross due to crop failure. There was, however, some hardship and distress due to the "improvements" and the letting of sheep runs, but if we except the so-called sheep "riot" of 1792, there was no real unrest. Indeed, there were few more law abiding and loyal subjects than the men of Easter Ross during this period. In 1794, when there was a great deal of disaffection and agitation in some other parts of the country, the Provost of Tain was raising a company of Tain volunteers to turn out "in Defence of His Sacred Majesty and the Laws and Liberty of our Kingdom."

In the Tain town council minutes of the day it is recorded that "The Council resolved that in the present situation of affairs they consider it their Indispensible duty to manifest their Loyalty to their King, and their firm attachment to the constitution of these Kingdoms as by law established, and their Determined Resolution to maintain and Support the Same with their lives and fortunes. . . . That for this purpose they will raise a Company of Infantry of the Respectable Inhabitants of the Burgh to Consist of one Captain, two Lieutenants, one Adjutant, or Sergeant Major, three Sergeants, three Corporals, one fife Drum and sixty private men to be ready to march at any time by the Lord Lieutenant of the County or his Deputy for this District to quell internal Commotions in the County wherever the same shall happen within six miles of the Burgh, or within the following limits, viz. as far as the point of Tarbat Ness at the East, the ferrys of Cromarty and Invergordon West and North, and in case of actual Invasion to be ready to march when required by the Lord Lieutenant or his Deputy, or any General office under whose Command they may be put, to any part of this Country."

Thus exhorted, the Incorporate Trades of Tain met in the town house, and "having taken under their consideration the serious aspect of the present times" . . . "unanimously agreed to raise a Company of Volunteers from among themselves consisting of sixty men, as they will not yield to any Town or Corporation South or North of them in point of loyalty. They engage to turn out two days each week in order to be trained for Service for Internal Defence, not only to oppose an Invading Enemy, but also to crush any appearance of Sedition and tumult so wofully present in these United Kingdoms. . . ."

Not only one, but two Companies of Tain

Volunteers were raised, and in September of 1795, Alexander Baillie of Tarrel, the retiring Provost, was warmly thanked by Sir Charles Ross, the newly elected Provost, "for the spirited manner in which, under the present authority, he raised, embodied, and in a great degree disciplined the two Companies of Royall Tain Volunteers, at once so honourable and beneficial to the Town. . . ."

It is not recorded if this eighteenth-century "Home Guard" was ever called upon to repress "sedition and tumult", but from all accounts, there was no real disturbance in Easter Ross during the closing years of the century, although times were still relatively hard and farmers were slow to recover from the effects of the famine years.

Conditions tended to improve with more enlightened methods of farming and improved communications. In 1803 Parliament gave a grant for the making of roads and bridges in the Highlands, and set up a commission for this purpose. By 1809 a stage-coach was running between Inverness and Tain three days a week and making the return journey on alternate days. It took a day to cover the 44 miles of road, but this, at the time, was considered something of an achievement.

No vehicular traffic, at this time, went north of Tain, but a serious drowning disaster, which occurred in the Meikle Ferry in 1809, stressed the clamant need for a road bridge between Ross and Sutherland, and probably hastened the decision to build one. An iron bridge between Ardgay and Bonar, designed by Telford, was completed in 1812-13, linking Tain with the north, and in 1819, a mail-coach began to run from Tain to Thurso with a daily service of mails.

The Meikle Ferry disaster occurred on the morning of 16th August, 1809. It was caused by the overloading of the ferry boat, which was crowded with people who were making their way to a market at Tain. The boat, loaded to the gunwales, was about half way across the ferry when it capsized and sank, throwing everybody into the water. Among those on board was Sheriff McCulloch of Dornoch, who, according to a witness, remonstrated strongly with the boatmen about the overcrowding, and even persuaded some passengers to leave the boat; but on being finally assured that there was no danger, the Sheriff reluctantly took his place with the rest. When the boat left the shore there were still over a hundred people on board, leaving the boatmen barely room to use their oars; but a breeze sprung up and the sails were hoisted. About half way across, however, the breeze died away and left the boat becalmed. Then a swell arose and she began to ship water and list dangerously.

One of the survivors gave the following account of the tragedy:

"The wind dying away and there being a considerable swell of waves in the Kyle, the sail was taken down. At this time the waves were breaking over the gunwales of the boat, and adding to the quantity of water already in the boat, which was now become about a foot in depth. They endeavoured to row, but could not get her on. Upon this the people began to be alarmed and called out to put about and return to the shore. This they were endeavouring to do, when the boat sank by the mere weight on board. As she sank, the people ran to one side, which occasioned her turning over, bottom upwards. . . ."

A relief fund known as the Meikle Ferry Fund was launched for the benefit of the bereaved families, and raised what was then the considerable sum of £3,300, and as a consequence, it is said, not one person had to apply for Poor Relief.

An official statement, in connection with the disbursement of this fund, states that 99 people were drowned, mostly from the parishes of Creich and Dornoch, and only 12 were saved. Among the drowned was Sheriff McCulloch.

The disaster made many people hesitate to cross the Meikle Ferry, and when the bridge at Bonar was constructed, the Ferry lost much of its traffic, for many people from the Creich and Dornoch areas preferred to take the long, but safer route, via Bonar, to the Tain markets. Any doubts they may have had about the strength of the new iron bridge were soon put to rest, for soon after it had been opened, an enormous mass of fir tree logs embedded in pack ice, floated down the river Oykell and dealt the bridge a tremendous blow. Shortly after this, a schooner drifted into it and carried away two masts; but under all this stress Telford's bridge stood fast — and thus it stood for nearly 80 years; then, in the year 1892, a tremendous flood surging down the river burst over the banks and swept the bridge before it. A new iron bridge was built with the minimum of delay, which has happily weathered storm and tide to the present day.

The Meikle Ferry, however, as of old, is still the shortest and more direct route north, and the prospect of bridging it has often been considered. What appears to have been a practical plan for a laminated wooden girder bridge to span the Firth was designed about 1830 by Robert Stevenson, of Bell Rock Light House fame. The bridge was never built, but a model of it is still to be seen in the Edinburgh museum.

With the advent of the stage-coach and the passage of wheeled traffic through the burgh, the magistrates of Tain found it necessary to give more attention to the upkeep and repair of the streets. The cleanliness of side roads, which up to the turn of the century had been treated in an extremely haphazard fashion, now also became a matter for concern.

A Tain Town Council minute of 1780 gives us some idea of the state of roads at that time. In this minute, the magistrates deplored the "inattentiveness of the inhabitants to repeated acts of Counsell with respect to allowing middings and other nuisances to remain before their doors and shut up the passages of the streets." They intimated that the town officers had authority "to seize and demolish carts found loose on the streets", and that Alexander McCulloch, factor of Balnagown was authorised "to carry off for use of his farm any dung heaps or dirt or ffulzie in the open streets. . . ." But even at the beginning of the next century, it appears that the situation was far from ideal, for a meeting of Tain Town Council in January of 1811 reported that "though the health of the inhabitants depended much upon cleanliness . . . the streets were kept in a dirty manner. . . ." The Council's measures this time, however, appear to have been effective, for an English visitor to Tain about eight years later remarked upon the cleanliness of the burgh. At the time of his visit Tain had just undergone a considerable face lift in the way of building and alteration, and would have been looking at its best in the early Autumn sunshine.

The Royal Burgh at that time was probably not unlike the older part of Tain as it is at the present day, with the High Street the axial centre, and two streets running parallel, connected by side roads. Some of the old houses have no doubt disappeared, but the street lines remain and the centre of the Burgh, then as now, was where the Tolbooth, Market Cross and Council Chamber now stand.

In the early part of the century, two burns or small rivers — now covered over — cut across the High Street and Tower Street on their way to the sea, and these were bridged over to permit traffic to cross.

That part of the Burgh which lay to the east side of the High Street burn is described grandly in a gazetteer of 1803 as a "suburb" of Tain. The gazetteer notes that "the town has lately received a considerable increase towards the east, where several acres of ground have been feud for building on the estate of Mr. MacLeod of Geanies. This suburb is separated from the town by a small river, over which is a handsome bridge. . . ."

In the first twenty years of the century there was a great deal of new building, using the honey-coloured sandstone quarried from Tain hill. One of the most notable of the new buildings was the handsome solidly built Royal Academy.

Tain Royal Academy was founded by Royal Charter in 1809, on the petition of 36 noblemen and gentlemen connected with Tain and the north of Scotland. The Town Council of Tain subscribed 100 guineas towards its cost, and Lord Ankerville gifted the large park where the building stands. The Academy, which was endowed, was opened in January 1813 with the purpose of providing "for the youth of the three northern counties a good education, founded on morality and religion, such as might be expected to produce the happiest fruits to themselves, their parents and connections, and contribute ultimately to the improvement of the country which gave them birth, and to the general advantage of the kingdom."

Shortly after the opening of the Academy another prominent building was under construction at the other end of the Burgh. This was the new parish church, which was opened in 1815 to accommodate a much larger congregation than the old St. Duthus Church, which hitherto had been used for public worship.

The new church was described by Robert Southey, who visited Tain in 1819, as "a handsome new kirk in a sort of Gothic, but looking as much like a castle as a church. . . ."

This building today no longer serves as a church, but has been converted into a Town Hall.

The year 1810 saw some building activity in the centre of the burgh. This was commenced as the result of a meeting of the previous year when Provost

Sir Charles Ross reported to his council that "a very great inconveniency arose to the town for the want of a proper Market Place for butcher meat, meal, fish and other articles; as all that was at present to answer the purpose of a flesh market was a small shed built at the end of the Tolbooth, not suitable for the purpose, and the places for the other markets equally inconvenient. . . . That it has been suggested to him that the property lying upon the south side of the High Street, and belonging to Mr. MacLeod of Cadboll . . . extending from the High Street in the north to the back street (Queen Street) at the south would be a very convenient and centrical situation for the purpose. . . ."

The Council agreed to feu the Market Street property, and the market buildings and stance were built in the following year. It is interesting to note that prior to the building of the market buildings that fish, meat and other perishable foods were sold at open booths on the High Street.

But James Cameron, surgeon in Tain, reporting about 1840, on the condition of the people of Tain, points out that the common food of the inhabitants was certainly not meat, but was "chiefly vegetables, consisting of potatoes, oatmeal porridge, cakes and brose. The labouring classes seldom tasted flesh or fowl except on particular occasions, such as weddings, christenings and funeral dinners, and on New Year's day, which was their only holiday. They were able occasionally to buy fish, which was both plentiful and cheap, salt herrings and dried fish in winter, and cod and haddock during the summer season." The potato was unquestionably the chief article of diet:

". . . and there is probably no part of the United Kingdom that produces potatoes more grateful to the taste, and of a more nutritious quality."

"Among the men in Tain the habit of snuff-taking was almost universal, and of those who did not take snuff, the greater part smoked the tobacco pipe having come more generally into use since the visitation of cholera in 1832."

The outbreak of cholera did more to improve the sanitation of the burgh than the oft-repeated regulations and injunctions of the magistrates. Butcher meat too long kept, and spoiled fish, in particular, were considered prejudicial to health. Ashpits and dunghills were removed, and the magistrates ordered that a bell man with horse and cart should be sent directly, to clean up the closes and wynds in Tain.

According to Chamber's *Gazetteer of Scotland*, written in 1833, it is stated that "Tain possessed a good Jail, a good Inn, and a good Academy." In that order!

It is probable that the jail was a splendid edifice, but as the town possessed sixteen inns and ale-houses, and the Parish of Tain, three, it is possible that Chamber's listed only the best of the inns. It is also probable that the only academy north of Inverness merited his attention as well, for in all, there were eight schools in Tain; they were the Royal Academy and the Grammar School; "two female day and boarding schools, one supported by the burgh funds, and the other private; two private English Schools; a private class for young children of both sexes; and a Gaelic Society School; in all eight and all except the last, situated in the town.,"

About $1\frac{1}{4}$ miles to the north of Tain is Glenmorangie Distillery. In a field to the south-west of the Distillery there is believed to be the only monument to Sir Walter Scott outside Glasgow and Edinburgh. It consists of a large granite boulder left there by a retreating glacier of the ice age. On the side has been chiselled the inscription: "The Immortal Walter Scott Ob. 1832".

It has been said that when Glenmorangie Distillery was being built in 1843, it was carved out by a stone-mason working at the Distillery, immortalising the great author of whom he thought highly.

One may wonder where the stone-mason who made the inscription on the Morangie stone, gained his passion for books; but stone-masons with a bent for books, headed by Hugh Miller were not so uncommon in the Highlands at this time.

One of the exports of Easter Ross, early in the 1850's, was whisky. It was exported to Leith and London by ship from Invergordon. A considerable quantity of grain was shipped annually from this port, and many bullocks, sheep and lambs were shipped to London.

Tain and district depended to a great extent, on communications by sea from Invergordon and Portmahomack. Round about 1840, the *Duchess of Sutherland* sailed once a fortnight from Invergordon to London; the *Brilliant* sailed regularly during the summer once a week between Invergordon, and Inverness, Aberdeen and Leith; and the *Velocity* once a fortnight.

From Portmahomack a considerable amount of

timber, chiefly fir, was sent to the north of England, and the quantity of grain exported from that port for London, Leith and Liverpool in 1839 was 3,003 quarters of various kinds.

The number of vessels that cleared from Portmahomack outwards since the 1st November, 1839 until the 1st November, 1840 was 113. The amount of tonnage being about 6,896.

Coal was imported from the north of England, and according to the *Second Statistical Account*, referring to Tain, the fuel generally used "except by those persons who reside near the peat mosses, is English coal, at the rate of 1/8d. per barrel (the herring barrel is the measure still employed). It is found cheaper than peat used alone; though a large quantity of peat is almost daily brought into town, for sale in small carts, chiefly from the neighbouring parish of Edderton, and is purchased to be used along with the staple fuel."

In 1868 the railway came to Tain, and in 1874 it reached Thurso. Passengers and goods arrived more quickly and more reliable than by ship. Also in 1874 the last stage-coach was driven from Inverness to Thurso. One of the drivers was George Ross, the descendants of whom live in Tain at the present day.

The Highlands at last were open to the south. The deer forests were created, but here there was little employment. Many Highlanders emigrated to England, Glasgow and abroad, and this little poem was written by W. A. MacKenzie, a native of Tain, exiled in London.

The nostalgia, which finds expression in his lines, will find a ready echo in the hearts of many who have strayed far away from "the little town between the heather and the sea," but who will ever look upon it as Home.

Far from here, where skies and streets
of sullen brown
    Darker seem than all things else that be,
Slowly smoke the little chimneys of a town,
    Set between the heather and the sea.
Heather! How the splendid purple of you
gleams
    Royally and proudly to the sun,
Fleeting through the moody greyness of
my dreams
    Ever till my web of dreams be done.
Sea! O sea that matched my tears with ebb
and flow,
    Sharer of my sadness and my mirth,
Well I know your call — Ah, sure well I know
    All the old friend voices of the Firth.
Little town! and far off little town of Tain!
    Grey and old, and wise as you are old!
Others come and look, and call you pauper plain,
    Cheerless, callous, comfortless and cold.
Others! blind and babblers all! Do I not
know —
    I that have been held against your
breast —
Drunken with your spring delight and winter woe,
    Drowsy with the magic of your rest —
You are lovely with a loveliness that grows
    Greater in despite of evil days,
Haloes you, and round you, as a girdle throws
    Beauty none may ever match with praise.
You, O little town! O grey and wrinkled town,
    Set between the mountain and the foam!
Shadow clear and clear on London's screen of
brown
    Heather wave and rooftree of you — Home!

Home is here. And yet — and yet — O little
place,
    Set between the heather and the sea,
Pale in winter wanness, flushed with summer
grace,
    Dear and dear and dear are you to me.

Tain, in the poet's fancy is matriarchal: "Grey, old and wise". But sometimes as she dreams in the sunlight she is golden and gay, and who dare guess her age? Some say that she has lived for more than a millennium, but like most ladies she is coy about her age. During her long lifetime she has known the confusion of wars and strife, but she has also known more temperate and moderate days. Time was too, when the vanquished and oppressed fled to her for protection, and her name was revered throughout the land.

Now, as though quietly reflecting upon these former days, she rests, gazing with quiet serenity at blue and distant hills, while ever present to stir up precious and half-forgotten memories, with their ceaseless gossip, are ". . . the old friend voices of the Firth".

Bibliography

ADAM, FRANK and INNES OF LEARNEY. The Clan Septs and Regiments of the Scottish Highlands.

ANDERSON, WILLIAM. The Scottish Nation. 1868.

ANDERSON, JOSEPH. Scotland in Early Christian Times. 1881.

BENTINCK, REV. CHAS. D. Dornoch Cathedral and Parish. 1926.

BROWNE, JAMES. History of the Highlands. 1839.

CHAMBERS. Domestic Annals of Scotland. 1859-61.

Culloden Papers. 1815.

DICKINSON, W. C. Scotland from the Earliest Times to 1693. 1961.

FERGUSON. The Dawn of Scottish Social Welfare. 1948.

FRASER, WM. The Earls of Cromartie, their Kindred, Country and Correspondence. 1876.

GORDON, SIR ROBERT. A Genealogical History of the Earldom of Sutherland. (Published from the Original Manuscript.) 1813.

HALDANE, A. R. B. The Drove Roads of Scotland. 1952.

HALDANE, A. R. B. New Ways Through the Glens. 1962.

JOHN EVAN. Crippled Splendour. 1938.

Kay's Original Portraits. 1837.

KELTIE, JOHN S. A History of the Scottish Highlands, Highland Clans and Highland Regiments. 1877.

MACCULLOCH, JOHN. The Highlands and Western Isles of Scotland. 1824.

MACGIBBON and ROSS. The Ecclesiastical Architecture of Scotland. 1896-97.

MACGILL, W. Old Ross-shire and Scotland. 1909. 1911.

MACKENZIE, W. C. The Highlands and Isles of Scotland. 1948.

MACKENZIE, MACKAY W. The Scottish Burghs. 1949.

MACKIE, R. L. King James IV of Scotland. 1958.

MACKINLAY, J. M. The Pre-Reformation Church and Scottish Place Names. 1904.

MACNAUGHTON, REV. COLIN. Church Life in Ross and Sutherland. 1915.

MACKINNON, DONALD. The Clan Ross. 1957.

MUNRO, ROBERT. Prehistoric Scotland. 1899.

MUNRO. Chronological and Genealogical Account of the Ancient and Honourable Family of Fowlis (taken from an ancient manuscript). 1805.

Old and New Statistical Accounts of Scotland (1st and 2nd).

PENNANTS. A Tour in Scotland. 1776.

Pococke's Tours in Scotland (Scottish History Society). 1887.

POLSON, ALEXR. Easter Ross. 1914.

RICHMOND, I. A. Roman and Native in North Britain. 1958.

ROLT, L. T. C. Thomas Telford. 1958.

ROSS, A. M. History of the Clan Ross. 1932.

SOUTHEY, ROBERT. Journal of a Tour in Scotland in 1819. 1929.

SKENE, W. F. The Highlanders of Scotland. 1902.

Stewart's Sculptured Stones of Scotland.

STUART, COLONEL DAVID. Sketches of the Character, Manners, and Present State of the Highlanders of Scotland. 1822.

TAYLOR, REV. W. History of Tain. 1882.

WAINWRIGHT, F. T. The Problem of the Picts. 1955.

WARRAND, DUNCAN. More Culloden Papers. 1925-27-29-30.

WATSON, W. J. Place Names of Ross and Cromarty. 1904.

WATSON, W. J. History of the Celtic Place Names of Scotland. 1926.

Further Reading

Tain Through the Centuries. By R. W. MUNRO and JEAN MUNRO. 1966.

Nigg. By W. R. I. NIGG. 1967.